OKINAWAN GOJU-RYU II

ADVANCED TECHNIQUES OF SHOREI-KAN KARATE

BY SEIKICHI TOGUCHI

OKINAWAN GOJU-RYU II

ADVANCED TECHNIQUES OF SHOREI-KAN KARATE

BY SEIKICHI TOGUCHI

Compiled by Toshio Tamano

Graphic Design by John Bodine

© 2018 Black Belt Books
All rights reserved
Printed in the United States of America
Library of Congress Number" 2001132529

First printing 2018 by

A Division of BLACK BELT MAGAZINE 1000

ISBN 0-89750-140-3

WARNING

MIDWEST CITY, OKLAHOMA

ACKNOWLEDGEMENTS

I would like to express my deepest thanks to Toshio Tamano and Scott Lenzi for their tireless efforts in the production of this book. I would also like to thank Geraldine Simon of Ohara Publications at Black Belt Communications, Inc. for her efforts in producing this book. It has long been my dream to present a book on Okinawan goju-ryu that demonstrates the advanced techniques and principles of the shorei-kan school of goju-ryu.

I feel that the shorei-kan system is the realization of a dream by my teacher, Chojun Miyagi. Within this system are the theories, principles and techniques I learned from him and Seko Higa, his top student.

Seikichi Toguchi

If you would like more information on shorei-kan, please contact:

In Europe:
Shihan Toshio Tamano, 8th Dan
c/o Shorei-Kan Europe
B.P. 112
37541 Saint Cyr Sur Loire, Cedex
France

In the United States:
Shihan Scott Lenzi, 6th Dan
Shorei-Kan USA Honbu Dojo
1062 Oregon Road, Cortlandt Manor, N. Y. 10567
(914) 739-7804
slenzi@warwick.net

DEDICATION

I would like to dedicate this book to my teachers, Chojun Miyagi and Seko Higa, for teaching me the happiness of goju-ryu karate.

ABOUT THE AUTHOR

Seikichi Toguchi was born on May 20, 1917, in Naha City, Okinawa. He studied karate under Chojun Miyagi and his assistant, Seko Higa. During World War II, Toguchi served the Japanese Imperial Army as an electrical engineer in Southeast Asia. He returned to Okinawa in 1946 to find the land barren and devastated, the people starving and depressed. Recognizing his homeland's need for vital reconstruction, he devoted himself to rebuilding Okinawa.

When a new *dojo* (training hall) was finally established, the Okinawan Athletic Association offered him a teaching position. He accepted and taught for two years in what was possibly the only karate dojo in post-war Okinawa at that time.

When Chojun Miyagi organized the Goju-Ryu Association in 1952 to oversee the establishment and maintenance of the *goju-ryu* style, Toguchi was named its executive director. Two years later, the Goju-Ryu Association became the Goju-Kai Federation and Toguchi was elected vice president.

Among the many honors received throughout his lifetime, Toguchi accepted an invitation by the Japan Karate Federation (JKF) to participate as the Okinawan master at its first opening demonstration and world karate tournament held in Tokyo, Japan, in 1969.

Shortly after completing this book, Toguchi died on Aug. 31, 1998, at the age of 81 and was unable to see it published. He is survived by his wife and son.

CONTENTS

Part I

A Martial Arts Retrospective

Chapter 1

A PERSONAL HISTORY OF OKINAWAN GOJU-RYU KARATE

Kanryo Higashionna

W hen I was 16, I joined the *dojo* (training hall) of Seko Higa. It was 1933 and I was at school for the study of fishery. The dojo was near my home and had been operating for about a year before I joined. Higa had opened the dojo after retiring from the police force.

Prior to starting my formal training with Higa, I had studied the fighting arts from my father, who had me practice daily on the *makiwara* (straw-padded striking post) in our backyard. I looked forward to formal training because I felt it would make me strong. As a boy, I had dreams of becoming a boat captain and felt that being strong would be a great asset.

There are many dojo in Okinawa now, but at that time there were very few. *Goju-ryu* karate dojo numbered only two: Okinawan goju-ryu founder Chojun Miyagi's dojo, located in the Matsuyama-cho section of

Chojun Miyagi

Naha city, and Seko Higa's dojo, located in the Kumoji section of the same city.

Although we called it a dojo, Miyagi actually trained in his garden. Higa's dojo was his living room and *roka* (hallway/foyer). It should be noted here that only three of Miyagi's students were certified to open a dojo: Seko Higa, Jinan Shinsato and Jinsei Kamiya.

This is confirmed in a 1936 article, "Karate Do Gairyaku," written by Miyagi. Although those three students taught and promoted goju-ryu, only Higa actually opened his own dojo and professionally taught the art. No other student of Miyagi ever opened a branch dojo while the master was alive.

In this article, Miyagi also named the following individuals as teachers of Okinawan karate: Kentsu Yabe, Chomo Hanashiro, Chotoku Kyan,

Seko Higa

Anbun Tokuda, Chohatsu Kyoda, Choshin Chibana, Jinsei Kamiya, Shinpan Gusukuma, Seko Higa, Kamado Nakasone and Jinan Shinsato.

When I joined Higa's dojo, there were only seven or eight students. I remember Seiju Yamashiro and Choboku Takamine were Higa's top students. Higa also had a female student named Hatsue Maeshiro who later became widely known as an expert with the *sai* (fork-dagger featuring two curved prongs).

Miyagi often came to supervise and teach at Higa's dojo. We were fortunate to be able to study with both masters.

EARLY BEGINNINGS

The first thing I learned from Higa was how to walk in the *sanchin dachi* (basic "hourglass" stance). This exercise was monotonous and boring

The author, 18 years old

but repeated numerous times until *sensei* approved. We were usually asked to perform *kata* (form[s]) in front of him one at a time. When he finished teaching one of us a segment of kata, he would call for the next student. Meanwhile, other students practiced by themselves in the garden either doing kata or practicing *kigu hojo undo* (equipment exercises), which consisted of makiwara, *sashi* (thrusting stones), *chishi* (circular block-like tools with handles) and *kongoken* (iron ring).

Over the course of many years, I learned each of the goju-ryu *koryu* (classical) kata one at a time. I learned them in the following order: *saifa* ("smash and tear"), *seyunchin* ("pull into battle"), *seisan* ("13 hands"), *seipai* ("18 hands"), *shisochin* ("conquer in four directions"), *sanseiru* ("36 hands"), *kururunfa* ("forever peacefulness, stops, shatter") and *suparinpei* ("108 hands"). It generally took one to two years to learn each kata. The most advanced kata of goju-ryu is suparinpei, which I learned after World War II.

Both Higa and Miyagi were very strict and questions were not permitted during training. When we practiced, we were not allowed to perform the kata beyond the part they had taught us. In essence, you were not allowed to learn a new sequence of the kata until the initial section or techniques were approved. However, we often learned these later sequences beforehand because our *sempai* (seniors) showed us.

Generally, *kumite* (sparring) was not taught until after 10 years of study, and no explanation of techniques was given. We simply followed instructions. We were not even permitted to utter a word in response to their commands during training. We heard only the voices of our masters. The sensei often said they were the "sculptors" and we were "the raw material" to be sculpted.

The main training subjects were the constant repetition of the *gekisai dai ichi** (attack and smash number one) and *gekisai dai ni* (attack and smash number two) kata, which were created by Miyagi. We also did *yobi undo*, a series of warming up exercises also created by Miyagi. This sequence involved a combination of karate techniques and yoga exercises designed to build our bodies for better performance of karate techniques. This beginning exercise sequence was regularly practiced for one hour in each class. In my *shorei-kan* classes over the years, I kept the essence of this exercise series, but it was limited to 30-40 minutes due to time constraints.

---

* Master Chojun Miyagi created kata gekisai dai ichi with the cooperation of Master Shoshin Nagamine (Shorin, Matsubayashi-ryu).

Chapter 2

CHOJUN MIYAGI
AND
SEKO HIGA

Kanryo Higashionna (third from left in the front row).
Chojun Miyagi (third from left in the rear row, cir. 1910).

SEKO HIGA

Seko Higa really loved karate, which was why he quit the police force and opened his dojo. He was a gentle, happy man. I studied with him for more than 33 years and in all that time he never got angry. However, when he taught he was just like Miyagi: very strict. He was highly dedicated to the preservation of goju-ryu techniques and would practice for many hours in front of a mirror to check himself. I never saw anyone else practice to this extreme.

Higa joined Kanryo Higashionna's dojo of *naha-te* when he was 14 years old. However, after only three years of studying with him, Higashionna passed away. Higa continued his study with his sempai, Chojun Miyagi, and trained with him until his death in 1953. For nearly 40 years, he dedicated himself to Miyagi, who was one of the most significant individuals in the early development of Okinawan goju-ryu karate. I truly believe he was the most beloved student of Miyagi.

Higa went to teach karate in Saipan in 1935 at the request of a friend. This venture did not turn out well and after two years he returned to Okinawa. I believe that if Higa had spent this time in Tokyo, the history of goju-ryu karate would probably be quite different today. While Higa was in Saipan, I ran the dojo and conducted all classes.

When Higa returned, I went to Tokyo to study for my electrical

In the second row, from left: Seko Higa, Taizo Tabara, Kenwa Mabuni, Chojun Miyagi, Chohatsu Kyoda, Jin-an Shinsato, Keiyo Matanbashi. Behind Miyagi: Genkai Nakaima (cir. 1924).

engineering license. Prior to my departure, Miyagi gave me a letter of introduction to Gichin Funakoshi, who would later become well known as the father of karate. I met Mr. Funakoshi in the Koishikawa section of Tokyo, where he lived. He welcomed me, offered dinner and we had a wonderful time speaking of karate.

When I passed the exam for electrical engineering, I worked at the Kawasaki Seitetsu steel mill for a while then returned to Okinawa. It was at this time in 1940 that Higa received the rank of *renshi* (equivalent to seventh dan) from Dai Nippon Butokukai (the largest martial arts organization recognized by the pre-war government). This was in recognition of his dedication to karate. It was only the second time that the organization ever gave a certificate to a *karateka* (karate practitioner).

The only other person ever to receive a certificate was Miyagi, who had obtained the title of *kyoshi* (equivalent to eighth dan) six years earlier. Since Dai Nippon Butokukai was dissolved in 1946 at the order of the occupying American force, I believe that nobody else in the karate world was given a title of karate mastership by the pre-war government martial arts body.

Meanwhile, World War II escalated and I was drafted into the military, during which time I served as an electrical engineer for the army and was stationed in Sumatra, Indonesia. On the army base, *sumo* (Japanese wrestling) was very popular and consequently a permanent *dohyo* (wrestling ring) was built. I practiced karate by myself there in the early morning.

Many army officers noticed my solo practice and one day they asked me to teach them. I obliged and soon began teaching a group of officers. Because of this relationship, I was treated very well and became the envy of many soldiers. Karate proved to be a benefit during my stay in Sumatra.

I recall an incident while in the army that gave me another reason to appreciate my karate training. One of my colleagues was an alcoholic who became violent after drinking. One day, to stop him from hurting anyone, I subdued him and tied him to a tree. He didn't appreciate this and formed a plan for revenge. A few days later, while sitting in one of the grass shacks where we ate and engaged in after-dinner conversation with my colleagues, I suddenly felt something cold on the back of my neck. Just as I shifted my body, a spear passed by my ear. I turned and saw my friend whom I had tied to the tree. I grabbed the spear, disarmed him and he was later arrested by the military police.

Another great debt I owe my karate training became apparent when we lost the war and became prisoners of the British army. We were confined to a small barren island near Sumatra. There were more than 1,000 of us with no food except for meager rations brought by the British that were not nearly enough for everyone's survival. We ate whatever we could find on the island: tree bark, grass roots, lizards, etc. Many people died of starvation.

I had maintained my stamina and would walk to the beach daily and catch fish, shellfish and other edible things. I am convinced that without my karate training, I may not have had the energy or will to survive. I often dream about this hellish nightmare.

Finally, a boat from Japan came and took us home to Okinawa in December 1946. Immediately upon my return, I went to visit Miyagi and Higa. They lived in Gushikawa, a city located in the middle of Okinawa near Koza. Both were elated to see me return unscathed from the battlefield. Those masters who survived the atrocities of the Okinawan war were exhausted and miserable, as were all of the surviving Okinawans. Higa was also affected by the war and was financially affected more so than Miyagi. Because the country was in disarray, he was unable to find work.

CHOJUN MIYAGI

I remember well my training with Miyagi, in particular the look of his eyes: They were very intimidating. After training he seemed to transform and become gentle and warm and would often speak about the history of karate, it's relationship with Buddhism and his ideas about the future of karate. It was obvious to me that he cared greatly about his art and speaking about it made him happy.

He was one of the first karate teachers to commence instruction after the war. Slowly his students began to return from the conflict, but unfortunately one of his most senior students, Jin-an Shinsato, did not.

Although Miyagi was adopted into one of the wealthiest families on Okinawa, the war destroyed his assets and wealth. He found it difficult to survive, but remained an honest and simple man despite his impoverished situation.

Miyagi was especially affected by the deaths of two daughters and a son. I suppose because of this incomprehensible tragedy, Miyagi's blood pressure rose and his health began to fail. Even though he was distraught, he had already begun to teach karate at the police academy in Gushikawa right after the war in 1946.

Before the war, Miyagi had incurred a monetary debt of 10 yen to a Mr. Maeda in Itoman. Miyagi believed that the war was no excuse for not repaying this small obligation. So strongly did he feel this that he traveled all the way to Itoman to pay back the debt. At that time, there was no public transportation, so I drove him to Itoman and then back to Naha. Mr. Maeda was obviously moved by this great man's concern and honesty.

After the war, all of Miyagi's students wanted to help our teacher and promote goju-ryu. So we planned and publicized a karate demonstration with the goal of raising money for Miyagi. Because of his fame, we decided to use his name in the expectation that many people would come to watch. With much excitement we told Miyagi of our plan. He told us, "Your idea is excellent, but I do not want to demonstrate." This was a real problem since we had already publicized that he would perform.

Rather than mislead the public, we abandoned the project. Miyagi was a man who despised the idea of making money through karate. He never charged instruction fees. We would pay him in other ways, usually by bringing gifts or doing things for him.

I hope that these descriptions of the episodes in Miyagi's life convey to you what a unique person he was. For him karate was sacred like a religion and he held it in higher regard than money.

REBUILDING

As I mentioned, World War II had severely affected Higa's finances. He was unable to find work and although he wanted to teach karate, there were no students. People were worried about simply surviving each day, not practicing karate.

Fortunately, upon returning from the war, I became moderately successful, which allowed me to help Higa. My business was somewhat unique. I had located downed airplanes off the coast of Itoman and peeled off the metal coverings. I then melted down the metal and poured it into a mold that was actually an army helmet. Then I fashioned pots for cooking. Many people came to buy these as kitchen utensils and soon I was able to employ a few people and buy an old truck. At this time I asked Higa to come and live with me.

While Higa was living with me, Seiyu (Kaka) Nakasone of *Tomari-te* (Tomari hand) introduced me to my future wife, Haruko. With Higa acting as an official matchmaker, we married.

In 1947, I suggested to Higa that the time was right to build his dojo. He agreed and we decided to seek the help of Dr. Jinsei Kamiya, one of the three students Miyagi allowed to teach his discipline. He was a medical doctor who owned a hospital. I visited his house and told him of the difficult situation that Higa was in and how I wanted to build a dojo for him. I asked if he could help us, hoping he might have some land that we would be able to use. He immediately agreed and gave us land in Itoman. I was grateful to him and touched by his generosity and respect for Higa.

I collected money from Higa's students to purchase materials and we built a small dojo for him. The dojo was completed by the end of 1947 and may have been the first karate school built in Okinawa after the war.

I mentioned earlier that I never saw Higa get angry, but I must admit that there was one time. It had to do with this new dojo. At night, a section of the single room became Higa's bedroom. There was a wooden pole that acted as a support for the curtain which was hung at night to make his bedroom. I felt that without the pole we would have much more room for training. One day while he was away I cut down the pole and removed it. When he returned and found I had cut it down, he was furious. It was the first and last time I ever saw him angry. I apologized and replaced it immediately.

At this time, Dr. Kamiya was also the president of the Itoman Athletic Association. Two years after the opening of Higa's dojo, he built a training hall for the association that featured the practice of judo and karate. I was appointed, with the recommendation of Miyagi and Higa, to the

At the opening ceremony of the dojo of Itoman Athletic Association (1949), in the circles: 1. Chojun Miyagi, 2. Shoshin Nagamine, 3. Jinsei Kamiya, 4. Seko Higa, 5. Seiyu (Kaka) Nakasone, 6. the author.

post of karate *shihan* (master teacher) of this new hall. The opening ceremony of this dojo was attended by many celebrated masters including Chojun Miyagi, Seko Higa, Seiyu (Kaka) Nakasone (Tomari-te) and Shoshin Nagamine *(shorin, matsubayashi-ryu)*.

In 1950, we got together and decided to build a house and a dojo in Naha for Miyagi since his house was destroyed during the war. We all ran around collecting money. Dr. Jinsei Kamiya, a respected and popular man, wrote a letter of solicitation and I carried it around seeking contributions. We did not get much money in Naha but were very successful in Itoman because at that time the people of Itoman were much more well off. We built a small house and a dojo for our teacher in 1951. The photograph in which Miyagi teaches the four of us was taken in this newly built dojo.

One day in 1952, after training with Miyagi and Higa, a number of us got together and discussed the idea of forming an organization to promote the growth of goju-ryu karate. We came up with the name Goju-ryu Shinkokai (association to promote goju-ryu). Miyagi agreed, and we began

In the new dojo of Miyagi (1952). From left: Meitoku Yagi, Chojun Miyagi, Eiichi Miyazato, the author and Eiko Miyazato.

preparations. The founding members were Seko Higa, Keiyo Matanbashi, Jinsei Kamiya and Genkai Nakaima.

We placed two announcements in the *Ryukyu Shinpo* newspaper: one invited all of Miyagi's students, past and present, to join; the second announced the actual establishment of the association.

Nakaima drafted the original rules and regulations for the association. As part of these guidelines, he detailed the rules for promotional examinations. At that time, Miyagi never gave his students any *dan* (black belt ranking). Since all of us wanted to wear black belts similar to those worn in judo, we supported Nakaima's inclusion of the dan system.

Once completed, we brought the charter to Miyagi for his approval. Upon reading the section dealing with dan ranking, he asked who would actually give this ranking. We responded that he, the style's founder, would do that. He got quite angry and said he would never give dan ranking to us. He said that the dan should only be given by the emperor's family via Dai Nippon Butokukai. We really couldn't argue the point as he was our teacher. We deleted the section pertaining to rank from the charter.

Since Miyagi died suddenly the following year, none of us received dan ranking from him. The truth of the matter is that we, his senior

In the garden of Miyagi's house (1952). In the rear row, third from left:
Eiichi Miyazato, Chojun Miyagi (sitting), Meitoku Yagi, the author and Eiko Miyazato.

students, promoted each other in an effort to promote goju-ryu.

Let me explain a little more on this matter. After our teacher's demise in 1953, we reorganized Miyagi's Goju-ryu Shinkokai and changed the name of the association to Okinawa Karate-do Gojukai (the association of Okinawan karate goju-ryu). The first president was Seko Higa. I was elected vice president. It was on this occasion that we granted dan rankings to each other. This association is still active in Okinawa.

Beginning in 1952, Miyagi's health severely declined. When he taught us, he always sat on a chair and orally instructed us one at a time. He would make comments such as: "Ah, the hand is too high, lower it," or "Bend your elbow and turn it inward." He would also have the senior students physically correct the juniors.

In the pre-war classes, Miyagi taught the sanchin kata with two 180-degree turns. However, after the war, he remained seated and would not allow students to turn their backs on him. It was considered disrespectful to turn one's back on their teachers in Okinawa. Thus, the turns were subsequently eliminated from the original form and what remained in their place were three steps forward and three back.

Therefore, the students who joined the dojo around 1950 learned this later version of sanchin. I have heard that some of these people mistakenly believe that this is the correct form of sanchin and even teach it as such. But let me emphasize: The technique of turning by the crossing of legs is critical to goju-ryu karate techniques. There are many turning techniques in the eight goju-ryu koryu kata. The fundamental kata — sanchin — without this proper turning technique, serves little purpose for advanced training. I regret that Miyagi changed the kata because it has caused much confusion in goju-ryu karate in Okinawa and throughout the world.

I would like to set the record straight with regard to sanchin kata. In Chojun Miyagi's article, "Goju-ryu Kenpo" written in 1932, he clearly explains the precise techniques of sanchin kata. In Miyagi's own words we can see the clarification and detail about turning and its importance. In the chapter "Explanation on the Basic Kata Sanchin" (See figure C.), he writes:

> The third important keypoint: After the third forward step and punch with left hand, pull the left hand back past your nipple and then bring it under the right elbow (your elbow is on top of the left wrist).
>
> At the same time you place your right foot diagonally in front of the left foot in order to be able to stand in correct sanchin dachi after turning (at this foot position the legs are crossed).

Then quickly turn on the ball of the foot as if you are pressing both feet into the ground. After completing the turn, execute a right-hand punch.

There is another important item I wish to clarify. Let me first say that I was not named the successor of goju-ryu by Miyagi, but nor was anyone else. There are some goju-ryu teachers who claim to have been privately appointed successor by Miyagi. These claims are ludicrous and disrespectful to his memory. He never publicly named anyone as successor. Common sense would dictate that if he were to appoint someone, it would have been to a longtime student and it would have to be of public record to have any value. Miyagi was not a man to do things in a haphazard manner — everything was very deliberate and precise.

It would also be logical to assume that since Miyagi would not grant dan ranking, how then would he be inclined to name a successor? I feel Miyagi would be rolling over in his grave with the plethora of ridiculous claims about this matter.

I believe that in the beginning of 1953, he felt death was near. His blood pressure was very high and I noticed that his strength and stamina were low. Looking back, I see now that with the approach of his death, he felt the time was right to impart his secret theories of karate to me. These theories included *kaisai no genri* (the theory on karate kata), how to create *hookyu* (unified) kata and the concept of creating and developing a teaching system for karate. These were all fundamental to create a legacy for future generations.

I cannot stress enough how puzzled I was that he discussed these things. Until this time he never taught theory. As I previously mentioned, Miyagi never explained what we did or the reason behind it. I was happy that he confided in me but was somewhat bewildered.

By 1953, I had a tea business. While on my deliveries, I would often stop at Miyagi's house to say hello. He would begin speaking of these theories and would go on for hours at a time.

Needless to say, I found it difficult to complete my delivery work. While he was speaking, I naturally could not leave. Many times his wife would come in and say, "Toguchi, sensei is tired. Perhaps it's time to leave."

Hearing this Miyagi would get angry and say, "I haven't finished my conversation yet. Leave us," and she would leave. I remember this fondly as it was a funny scene. It was obvious to me by his actions and passion that he really wanted to transfer his valuable information to me.

He died on Oct. 8, 1953, of heart failure. The death of my teacher was a great shock to me. After his death I wondered why he apparently gave this information only to me. I thought about it constantly for days and weeks and finally came to the realization that it was my teacher's wish that I complete his dream of creating a karate teaching system.

Upon my master's death, I wrote a commemorative poem:

> *A tiger dies and leaves its fur,*
> *A man dies and leaves his name,*
> *A teacher dies and teaches death.*

剛柔流振興會設立總會

剛柔流型手道の振興を圖る爲、宮城長順
先生に直接又は間接に師弟の關係あるの
が協力結集してここに設立總會を開催す
ることにいたしました、關係者並に御贊
同御支援の方々の御參集をお願いいたし
ます

記

一、期日　六月一日（日曜日）午後一時
一、場所　菊之家旅館（市場交番から浮
　　　　　島通への角）
一、會費　二五〇円

發起人代表

比嘉世幸
眞玉橋景洋
神谷仁清
仲井間元楷

中込　那覇市六區一組
　　　仲井間元楷方

(Figure A)

The notice of a meeting to discuss establishing the association of Goju-ryu Shinkokai in *Ryukyu Shinpo* newspaper (1952).

It reads:

The general assembly for founding Goju-ryu Shinkokai.
In order to promote the growth of goju-ryu karate, those who directly or indirectly study with Chojun Miyagi will hold a general assembly to establish the association Goju-ryu Shinkokai. We need your support and hope you join us.

Date: June 1st (Sunday), 1 p.m.
Place: Kikunoya Ryokan (hotel)
Fee: 250 yen

The founding members:
Seko Higa
Keiyo Matanbashi
Jinsei Kamiya
General Nakaima

Office:
Genkai Nakaima
1 Kumi 6 Ku, Naha city

(Figure B)

The notice in *Ryukyu Shinpo* newspaper of Goju-ryu Shinkokai having been founded.

It reads:

The announcement of establishment of Karate-do Goju-ryu Shinkokai.
We have founded Goju-ryu Shinkokai for the purpose of preserving traditional karate and promoting the growth of the discipline worldwide. We do our best for the art and look forward to having support from the people who are concerned with us. July 2, 1952

President of Goju-ryu Shinkokai
Chojun Miyagi

The chief of the board of directors
Genkai Nakaima

Information and inscription:
Starting from July 1 classes are 4 times a week. (Monday, Wednesday, Thursday & Saturday) anyone wishing to study contact:
Genkai Nakaima
1 Kumi 6 Ku, Naha city
The office of Karate-do Goju-ryu Shinkokai - Tel. 145

Branch dojo in Koza city
Seisho Inamine
3 Han Yaejimaku, Koza city

Figure C. The cover of the article "Goju-ryu Kempo." The letters are Chojun Miyagi's own handwriting.

It reads:

To Mr. Kiju Azama
August 29, 1932   Chojun

Goju-ryu Kempo

Chapter 3

DEDICATION, DEVOTION AND COMMITMENT

I felt strongly that it was Miyagi's desire that I complete his dream. Taking this very seriously, I quit my business and opened a dojo in Koza city as a full-time professional karate teacher. I opened my shorei-kan dojo in March 1954. I believe that it was the third dojo to open after the war in Okinawa after Higa and Miyagi's schools. I had only a few students in the beginning, so my wife worked to help support us.

Koza city was the home of the United States Air Force base at Kadena and many American soldiers came to the dojo for instruction. At first I had hostile feelings toward Americans so I refused to teach them. Then one day, a student of Higa introduced me to an American soldier and

Shorei-kan dojo in 1954. Center: the author, right: Ryugo Sakai.

asked me to teach him; this I could not refuse. After teaching him the word spread and I was soon teaching about 40 American soldiers.

Looking back, I realize that teaching the American GIs really helped me to apply Miyagi's theories while developing a cohesive teaching system. Had I not taught them, my shorei-kan system would look nothing like it does today. This may sound confusing, but let me explain. When I taught kata to the Americans, they always asked questions regarding the meaning of the kata movements and how they could be applied to real fighting situations. Okinawans would never ask such questions. I could not speak English, so I spent countless hours figuring how to clearly transmit the meanings of the kata. Since kata is like a dance form and the techniques of combat are contained within, I thought that a two-person sequence of the kata would give clear answers to the questions posed by the Americans.

I named this subject *bunkai kumite* (two-person sequence of kata). The first one I created was for Miyagi's gekisai dai ichi kata that I illustrated in my previous book *Okinawan Goju-ryu* (Ohara Publications Inc., 1976). I found that by practicing this they could learn and develop the basic techniques of karate: timing, focus, power and speed.

The author training with American soldiers (1957).

However, as time passed, I found that this sequence was difficult for beginners, so I created an easier version of kumite called *kiso kumite* (systematized pre-arranged sparring) which provided a more progressive method of learning karate techniques. I found that this worked very well, so I created 10 levels of kiso kumite.

Miyagi's lifelong goal was to make karate part of the physical education curriculum in schools. For this reason, he believed it was of the utmost importance to develop a group teaching method. This concept is clearly detailed in his article "Karate-do Gairyku" in the section entitled "Karate Teaching Method."

This section illuminates several components of his view on teaching karate systematically:

- *yobi undo* (warming up exercises)
- *kihon kata* (basic kata: *sanchin, tensho, naifanchi*)
- *hojo undo* (supplementary exercises, including basic techniques and equipment)
- *kaishu kata* (classical kata)
- *kumite renshu* (sparring exercises)

Miyagi once told me of his idea to make 10 new hookyu kata. Unfortunately, he died after only creating gekisai dai ichi and dai ni kata.

After a goju-ryu karate demonstration in Itoman (1957). In the front row from left: Seiko Kikuchi, George Kobayashi and Juei Tamashiro. In the rear row: the author, Koshin Arashingaki, Seko Higa, Meitoku Yagi, Yushin Tamashiro and Choshi Ishimine.

He had also told me of his ideas for making the next advanced set of kata, which he called the *gekiha* (advanced kata) series. So, following his principles, I created the gekiha dai ichi and dai ni kata. I showed them to my teacher Higa and my sempai Mr. Meitoku Yagi. They both approved and felt it was what Miyagi sensei was striving for. This made me very proud and I continued to create kata, numbering eight in all, adding them to my teacher's original two. I believe I have fulfilled his dream of making 10 hookyu kata.

In addition to these kata, I created other subjects. It took more than 20 years to complete the shorei-kan karate teaching system. As can be seen by reviewing Miyagi's "Karate Do Gairyaku" article, my shorei-kan system follows the precepts and principles set forth by my teacher.

I am proud to say that I have added a new dimension to Okinawan karate with my teaching system. The following is an excerpt from an article written for our 1970 school newsletter by Ryugo Sakai, one of my first students.

> At that time, the dojo was very small with a training floor of about 30 square meters. After each night's training, Toguchi sensei always talked to us about his vision of karate for the future under the beautiful starry sky until late night.
>
> In these early days of karate, people still called the discipline te and it was taught in the old fashion manner. No master of a karate dojo on Okinawa employed a promotional system and only teachers put black belts on themselves.
>
> It was Toguchi sensei who initiated a teaching method of karate including the promotional system. Many karate teachers from all styles criticized him for his endeavor. Toguchi sensei ignored them. He made the belt system with four colors: white, green. brown and black. I still clearly remember the excitement of changing the belts after I was promoted each time.
>
> In 1956, an all-Okinawan athletic festival was held in Koza city. Each dojo sent five karateka to demonstrate. All of them, tough looking guys with more than 10 years of experience in karate, did very impressive kata and budo kumite whereas we, with merely three years of experience, demonstrated the subjects Toguchi sensei created for his system.
>
> All participants were anxious to read the following day's newspapers. We wanted to know which school would be in the headlines. And it was shorei-kan. The two major newspapers of

the island showcased shorei-kan in their papers with big and numerous photos.

Since then, the fame of shorei-kan spread in the Okinawan karate world. At the aforementioned festival, Master Shoshin Nagamine (shorin, matsubayashi-ryu) praised Master Toguchi as one of the greatest karateka in the history of Okinawan karate.

Shortly after the festival, many dojo began their own promotional system."

I must note here another important experience that aided me in the development of the shorei-kan karate teaching system. Until around the time I opened my dojo, there existed a custom on Okinawa between karateka to test each other's fighting skills in actual combat. This custom was called *kakidameshi*.

The more famous the karateka, the more often he would be challenged by a karateka seeking fame. Seiyu (Kaka) Nakasone of tomari-te was a carpenter by trade. He was once attacked by a man while working. Nakasone instantly blocked the assailant's attack and simultaneously struck the man on the head with the hammer he was holding. The man

The demonstration in Koza city (1956). Center: Ryugo Sakai, far right: Joe White (an American soldier).

was knocked unconscious and hospitalized.

Seko Higa and Choshin Chibana of shorin-ryu were constant targets of kakidameshi. I was challenged quite often and therefore always walked close to the left side of the road so as to never leave my left side open. I became especially careful at corners, where attacks often occurred. When I went home late at night, I would first knock on my door to let my family know I was approaching. I would then walk around the block once, watching in all directions, and would enter my home through the back entrance. Nowadays these attacks seem unbelievable, but it was a true part of karate life in Okinawa back then.

It is very interesting to note that Chojun Miyagi was an exception to kakidameshi. Even though he was very famous, he was held in great respect and awe by all karateka on Okinawa and thus no one dared to test his fighting skill. Of all the teachers I have known, none was respected like Miyagi. This was truly remarkable.

With regard to kakidameshi, I would like to describe one of my experiences. As I mentioned earlier, when I opened my dojo in Koza city, my wife helped support me by running a shop. One day some *yakuza* (gangsters) came to her shop to extort money. I naturally refused their demands. As expected, they challenged me to kakidameshi. All yakuza on Okinawa practiced karate and they were eager to test my skills. Approximately a dozen men came to the shop armed with clubs. I luckily beat them all and they were subsequently arrested.

I always kept in mind these real fighting situations as I was developing my shorei-kan teaching method. Utmost in my mind was that the techniques studied had to actually work in a real fighting situation.

Miyagi always said that *budo* (martial ways) had to really work in the streets. In his article "Karate Do Gairyaku," he describes the term *kaisai*, which simply means the applications hidden in koryu kata. The heart of this kaisai theory, as described by Miyagi, is *kobo no jitsu* (the essence of fighting). This term means that in a real street fight, the application taken from koryu kata must really work. This is a point he describes clearly in his article. Although I never looked for a fight, I was often forced into one. In the frequent engagement of kakidameshi, I gained great insight and experience that helped me in developing the shorei-kan system.

A FEDERATION BEGINS

During these years, life was difficult for the Okinawan people and very few practiced karate. Even so, in 1956 the Okinawan Karate-Do Federation was established. The first president was Choshin Chibana (shorin-ryu) and the vice president was Seko Higa. In addition to Shoshin Nagamine (shorin, matsubayasi-ryu), Yuchoku Higa (shorin-ryu) and I were appointed to the board of directors. This was perhaps the first time karate people in Okinawa united.

When I opened my dojo, many Okinawans were poverty-stricken. My respected friend, Shinken Taira of Okinawan *kobudo* (weapons way), was among those devastated by the war. Once I had enough students, I invited him to teach kobudo in my dojo. Even after I left Okinawa for Tokyo, he remained to continue teaching at my dojo.

Taira taught there for almost five years. Using his kobudo techniques, I created the shorei-kan subjects rhythm *bo dai ichi* (staff kata number

The karate masters of Okinawa (1957). In the first row from left: Meitoku Yagi, Shoshin Nagamine, Hiroshi Kinjo, Choshin Chibana, Seko Higa, Yuchoku Higa. In the second row: Seiko Kikuchi, Kan-ei Ueichi, Katsuyu Miyahira, Jokei Kushi. In the third row: Kokichi Nagamine, Choboku Takamine, George Kobayashi, Shugoro Nakasato, Yoshio Shimabukuro, Choki Ohta and the author.

one performed to music) and *bo dai ni* (staff kata number two performed to music). I also incorporated several kobudo subjects and included weapons: *bo* (staff), sai, *tonfa* (Okinawan farming tool), *nunchaku* (two rods joined by short chain or rope), *kama* (sickle), plus others. Taira's involvement with shorei-kan is an important event that contributed to the development of my system.

With regard to music kata, I created the 10th hookyu kata to be performed to music. I named it *hakutsuru no mai* (dance of a white crane). I also created kata done to music which I named rhythm karate dai ichi, dai ni and dai san for children. All music for my karate and kobudo kata were composed by my friend Mr. Seihin Yamauchi, the renowned Okinawan folk music composer.

At this time, just after World War II, Okinawa was cut off from communication with mainland Japan. Consequently we had no knowledge

In the front row from left: George Kobayashi, Masao Mikami, the author, Seikichi Higa (son of Seko Higa). In the rear row: Seiko Kikuchi, Seko Higa, Kogyu Tazaki, Shinken Taira and Shunshin Furuken (1959).

of what was occurring with karate there and they had no knowledge of us. Because of this, I was chosen as the Okinawan Karate-Do Federation's representative to go to Japan in 1959 and ascertain the status of karate.

Surprisingly, what was being taught in goju-ryu dojo in mainland Japan was very different from Miyagi's teachings. This spurred a tremendous feeling of responsibility to teach original Okinawan goju-ryu karate in Tokyo. I realized that in order to follow Miyagi's dream to spread karate to the world, I would need to be in Japan. Therefore, I returned to Okinawa to make preparations for a move into Tokyo. I left my family in Okinawa along with my dojo that by then had 200 students, placing my two senior students in charge.

I first taught at a dojo in the Yoyogi section of Tokyo. I left after about a year and began teaching at several Shinto shrines. These classes were held outdoors and the summer brought many students while the winter drew very few. It was a very difficult time financially, but I felt strongly about my mission to spread traditional goju-ryu karate.

Chohatsu Kyoda and the author
(in Kyoda's house in Ohita-Kan, Japan 1958).

The winter brought little remuneration and training outside in the snow was both a new and unwelcome experience. After all, I had lived in warm Okinawa all my life. As I look back now, I recall it fondly, but it didn't seem so wonderful then.

In 1964, Seko Higa died. His death touched me more deeply than the death of Miyagi. We were like a family and our close relationship had ingrained in me a sincere and unique devotion to karate. I am who I am today because of my relationship with Higa.

Both Miyagi and Higa were karate *bushi* in the true meaning of the word. The term "karate bushi" is the highest term of respect in Okinawa for a karateka. I was very fortunate to have had them as my teachers and will be forever grateful.

In 1968, I was finally able to open an indoor karate dojo. I must note that this school — in the Nakano section of Tokyo — was built because of the dedication and enthusiasm of my students. This dojo was built for me just as we, the students of Miyagi and Higa, had built the dojo for our teacher. Most notable of my students is Toshio Tamano, whose father, Genkichi Tamano, built the dojo.

All of my students worked extra jobs and canvassed Japan and Okinawa in an effort to raise money to maintain the *honbu* (headquarters) dojo in Tokyo. With the Tokyo and Okinawa honbu dojo as the foundation,

In a Shinto shrine yard in Tokyo after a shorei-kan demonstration (1967).

shorei-kan began to spread to the United States, Europe, South and Central America, Canada, India and elsewhere around the world.

I would like to continue my mission to bring Miyagi's dream to the world. My life has been intertwined with goju-ryu karate for almost 65 years. I hope my recounting of it has provided you with insight and perhaps some inspiration.

Author (center) with senior students Toshio Tamano and Scott Lenzi outside Tokyo honbu dojo (1997).

Part II

The Secrets of Kata

Chapter 4

THE IMPORTANCE OF KATA AND KAISAI

KARATE KATA

Why is the solo activity "kata" — a dance-like movement — so important to the fighting art of karate? Although this question is very important and quite common, I do not believe it has been explained from the traditional karate point of view by any Okinawan karate teacher.

Kata has two purposes: the practice of budo and a means of physical conditioning while executing those movements. There is a difference between sports movements and budo.

Generally speaking, physical movements for sports are based on those of daily life such as walking, running, throwing, jumping, lifting, etc. In sports, we compete using these familiar movements. How fast can we run? How much weight can we lift? How high can we jump? With this underlying concept integrating competition and personal challenge, man created the games of the marathon race, weightlifting, high jump, and so forth.

I believe the techniques used in sport karate are not very different from the movements of everyday life. Many of the punches and kicks used in karate *jiyu kumite* (free sparring) are easily copied and executed by children who have never studied the discipline. There is no consistent training required to execute these techniques. If you are big and forceful, you have an advantage in this type of sparring. If you can also execute swift attacking techniques, you can generally win.

The techniques of Japanese budo, however, are quite different from sport. When fighting with the techniques of the martial arts, you are not necessarily big and swift. Instead of using only your own speed and force, you are required to also utilize your opponent's power and speed. In doing so, however, you need to move in particular ways that are rarely found in everyday life.

In the koryu kata of goju-ryu, for example, there are many strange movements to which our bodies are not accustomed. That is why Miyagi created yobi undo, which was designed to get our body accustomed to such movements. And he augmented this training with *kigu hjo undo* (special equipment exercises) to improve the basic techniques and physical strength. By practicing these supplemental exercises, we can achieve the physical conditioning and flexibility required to learn and execute the koryu kata techniques.

Once our body is conditioned and we can perform kata techniques correctly, we are then ready to learn how to fight with budo techniques. This is why Miyagi taught kumite techniques only to those who could perform kata well.

Let me explain it more by applying a specific technique of goju-ryu's sanchin dachi and its walking pattern as an example. Sanchin dachi is the fundamental stance of goju-ryu karate. Each step consists of two movements:

1. Step with the toes of both feet pointed inward/heels outward while knees are slightly bent. The front foot's heel and the rear foot's big toe are on one line. The stance is approximately equal to your shoulder width. (See diagram A.)

(diagram A)

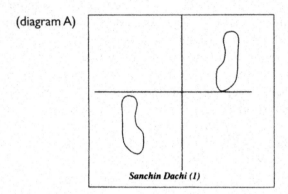

Sanchin Dachi (1)

2. Turn on the balls of both feet to bring your heels inward and your hips upward. When stepping, you slowly and alternately bring each foot forward or backward in a semi-circular motion. (See diagram B.) (Please refer to my book *Okinawan Goju-ryu* for more details on this stance).

(diagram B)

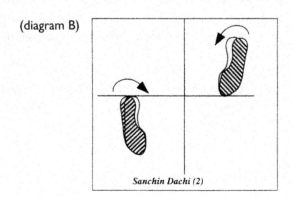

Sanchin Dachi (2)

It is indeed a strange stance and way of walking. No one would stand or walk in this fashion in normal life. And if we did so in an actual fight, we would surely and instantly be knocked to the ground.

Why then, do we use this clumsy footwork in goju-ryu karate? The answer is that this stance (and its semi-circular walking motion) was created as a training method to learn how to stand firmly while fighting. It is purely a training method, not something we apply in combat.

The semi-circular motion of the feet facilitates the proper alignment of the feet: toes inward/heels outward. Only after placing the feet in this position can we stand firmly by turning the heels inward while turning the hips upward. Though sanchin dachi is narrow and short, we can keep good balance while maintaining *ki* (energy) in the *tanden* (abdomen).

However, since this type of stance does not exist in daily life, it is very difficult for us to do without practice. We need to train our bodies to make it feel natural. That is why Higa insisted that I practice only this walk for three months when I joined his school.

Once we can correctly stand in sanchin dachi at any moment, in any circumstance, we no longer need to step in a semi-circular motion. We are then ready to learn other more advanced fighting techniques.

This training method is similar to that of learning a musical instrument. In playing the Okinawan *shamisen* (guitar-like string instrument), for example, the fingers of both hands move in different directions at different speeds simultaneously. We do not move our fingers this way in our daily life. So, as beginners, we learn a variety of fingering patterns and scales which we must practice every day. When our fingers can move smoothly, we are ready to learn to play music. This is exactly the same principle when learning goju-ryu techniques.

In this regard, there are some problems in the present karate world. Some karateka change kata of their styles into simplified movements. In other words, they transfer the kata's particular budo movements into those of daily life. By doing this, however, one can no longer condition oneself for budo techniques. Worse yet, the precious ancient techniques hidden in kata disappear.

That's why Miyagi and Higa were careful and strict in teaching kata. I, too, teach the same way because I believe it is my mission to transmit the valuable techniques of goju-ryu karate unchanged to future generations.

KAISAI

Let us examine the second purpose of karate kata training: the practice of secret ancient fighting techniques.

Kata is composed of many apparent movements of fighting techniques or *hyomengi*. However, we should be aware that many of them are modified movements of real fighting techniques. We need to research and find out the original fighting techniques created by ancient masters in kata's hyomengi by using a certain method.

The work to find hidden techniques in kata is called kaisai in goju-ryu karate. The guiding principle for kaisai is called kaisai no genri or "the theory of kaisai." These terms were created by Chojun Miyagi. He originally called kaisai *toki to musubi*, and kaisai no genri *toki to musubi no genri*. These terms are found in his aforementioned two articles "Karate-Do Gairyaku" and "Goju-Ryu Kempo." As he found the latter quite wordy, he changed them to the former. "Kaisai" and "toki to musubi" mean exactly the same in Japanese. A technique found from a hyomengi through the work of kaisai is called *kaisaigi*.

Many years ago, karateka were quite strict about keeping their own fighting techniques secret from other schools. As kata gradually were taught to a great number of people, the ancient masters knew it was difficult to conceal their kata from the eyes of other schools. So they orally transmitted the theory to only one student in each generation. Thus, they believed that even if kata were stolen, but the theory on how to read hyomengi's implication was not, the secrets would remain intact. Because of this reason, the theory of kaisai was never revealed to the public.

Chojun Miyagi taught me this theory just before his death and recommended that I not make it public. However, as karate has become popular around the world, I felt it would not benefit true karate if I were to hide it as a secret in my shorei-kan school. I regret that the public has lost confidence in traditional Okinawan karate and may not understand the true value of karate kata.

Hence, I would like to reveal a part of this theory for the first time while conveying to the reader the depths of Miyagi's goju-ryu karate. It should be noted that my student Toshio Tamano, with my permission, has written a book in Japanese on this subject titled *Okinawa Karate Goju-ryu, Shinjinbutsu Ohraisha* that was published in 1991.

Chapter 5

THE
EVOLUTION
OF KATA

Before examining kaisai no genri, one should understand how kata was created and how it evolved into its present form. In the beginning, ancient people created their own fighting techniques in the forms of two-man tandem sparring sequences. This type of kumite consisted of one or two techniques.

Through the ages, many techniques were created and the kumite were collected in great number. However, martial artists began looking for another way to train because they had difficulty remembering all the kumite. They also found kumite practice somewhat inconvenient because it regularly required a practice partner. Thus they sought a better way.

After centuries of trial and error, the people created a new training method: a solo, dance-like form. They changed some of the original kumite techniques into modified movements to fit a solo performance and hide the techniques from the eyes of the other schools.

In the primitive stage of kata development, techniques were randomly combined into a string of motions. In so doing, it became endlessly long and diffused from the choreographic point of view. The ancient masters were not satisfied with it.

As kata evolved, the masters painstakingly developed a set of regulations or guiding parameters. They did not simply combine techniques haphazardly but followed the rules to create kata. Consequently, they succeeded in making kata concise and easy-to-remember. The koryu kata of goju-ryu belongs to this evolved form.

So if we know those guidelines, we can guess how the ancient masters developed kata from the original fighting techniques. The rules they used were the prototype of kaisai no genri.

Kaisai is the process enabling one to trace the original technique hidden in the current-day koryu kata with the help of theory. Kaisai no genri is a kind of key to read a secret code.

KAISAI NO GENRI

Kaisai no genri consists of *shuyo san gensoku* (three main principles) and many *hosoku joko* (supplemental principles). For this publication, only shuyo san gensoku will be discussed.

The three main principles or shuyo san gensoku are:

1. **Don't be deceived by the Enbusen Rule.**
2. **Techniques executed while advancing imply attacking techniques. Those executed while retreating imply defensive or blocking techniques.**
3. **There is only one enemy and he/she is in front of you.**

Let us examine each of those principles in detail:

1. Don't be deceived by the Enbusen Rule.

Enbusen literally means the lines for performance of fighting techniques. (See diagram C.) The Rule of Enbusen was created in order to make kata concise. This was the first rule the ancient masters created for the last stage of kata.

Looking at the enbusen diagram, you will notice eight directions indicated by straight lines. The crosspoint of four lines is called the *kiten* (basic point). Kata is arranged to start at this point and move toward any of those eight directions and finish on or around kiten.

In the Rule of Enbusen, the stepping patterns are designed to be symmetrical. For example, three steps forward are countered with three

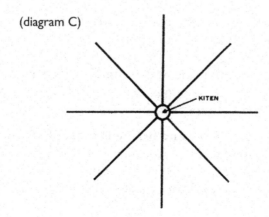

(diagram C)

KITEN

steps backward. One step left is balanced with one step rightward and so on.

Also, in order to keep kata concise, the ancient people limited the numbers of *unsoku* (footsteps) at a time. Normally, in Okinawan karate kata, we find the maximum number of unsoku is three.

In short, the movements in kata are regulated and artificially designed. The first rule of shuyo san gensoku is saying that those movements have nothing to do with real fighting situations. In a real fight, no one would step back because he/she advanced previously nor limit his/her number of steps to three. In a street fight, needless to say, every technique must be free, fast and, most importantly, spontaneous.

Therefore, applying kata movements directly to kumite is a mistake. A man performs a kata alone. His partners surround him in the directions of enbusen lines. When the center man executes the kata, his partners punch, kick or block according to the hyomengi he does.

We must remember that kata is choreographed and artificial. Punching left does not mean you fight against an enemy on your left side. The people who created this kind of kumite are fooled by the Rule of Enbusen. From training such as this, we'll never get kobo no jitsu from kata.

2. Techniques executed while advancing imply attacking techniques. Those executed while retreating imply defensive or blocking techniques.

If kata's hyomengi are not for real fights, how then do we find clues of real fighting techniques in it? The second rule gives us the answer. It says that when unsoku is in advance, we should always consider the real meaning of hyomengi as an attacking technique even if it appears to be a blocking one. When unsoku is in retreat, it should be considered a blocking technique even though the hyomengi is apparently an assault.

For example, in the seyunchin kata, there are *gedan uke* (low blocks) with advance steps in *shiko dachi* (square stance). According to the second rule, we must consider their kaisaigi as gedan striking techniques. If we ignore the rule and assume the gedan uke as they appear, we end up finding the opposite fighting techniques from the ones intended by the ancient people.

3. There is only one enemy and he/she is in front of you.

In kata, as we face toward many directions along the lines of enbusen, we tend to believe that kata is created in a situation wherein one man fights against several people at a time. Not so, the third rule says.

The origin of kata was a two-man tandem sparring form, as I have explained previously. It was the kumite of one vs. one. Therefore, when the ancient people rearranged it into a dance-like kata, they maintained its original concept of man-to-man combat.

In reality, from the street-fighting point of view, it is impossible to make a kata that is designed to fight against many attackers at once. A man cannot simultaneously execute many different techniques. This kind of fight exists only in movies or novels.

The third rule also says when doing kaisai, we should, as a principle, consider the imaginary opponent as always in front of us and look for a kaisaigi accordingly. Though we do find kaisaigi in some kata fighting against an enemy behind us, the majority of them are the ones against an adversary in front.

With the main three principles of kaisai no genri, we can roughly guess a kaisaigi of a hyomengi. In order to find a precise one (or many), we need to use the regulations of hosoku joko. However, since my space within this book is limited, such a topic would require further analysis elsewhere.

THE METHOD OF KAISAI

There are two methods in kaisai. Chojun Miyagi named them *en-eki-ho* (deductive method) and *kino-ho* (inductive method).

En-eki-ho is the method in which we deductively find kaisaigi from hyomengi. It is the way to logically analyze a specific hyomengi of a kata and find its kaisaigi by following the rules of kaisai no genri.

For example, we try to figure out the meaning of the hyomengi at the beginning of the seipai kata in which we swing the right arm in a semicircular motion in *shuto uchi* (knife-hand strike) fashion. We utilize shuyo san gensoku and hosoku joko and logically find the answer.

Kino-ho is a method to inductively search for some fighting techniques usable to a particular fighting situation in hyomengi kata. This method resembles the solving of a mathematical problem. A kata is like a mathematical formula or equation with a specific fighting situation being similar to a number or value we would insert into the math formula. We solve the mathematical equation by inserting a numeric figure into the formula. In the same fashion, we search for a kaisaigi by applying a specific fighting situation to kata.

By using either one of those two methods, we try to find a kaisaigi. However, the work of kaisai is not completed at this stage. After finding what one believes to be a kaisaigi or application, one must examine it to see if it is an effective technique for actual combat. For this, we rearrange the newly found kaisaigi into a two-man tandem kumite, which is called kaisai kumite. It is, in effect, the reverse of the evolution of kata to find a kumite's origin from a kata we practice today.

Once we are sure that the kaisaigi works, we must practice this kumite over and over until we master it. When we reach a level in which we can freely use the technique, as Miyagi writes in his previously mentioned articles, we have obtained kobo no jitsu. The work of kaisai finishes here.

I would like to note that I used both methods to find many kaisaigi in the koryu kata of goju-ryu and used them to create all subjects of *yakusoku kumite* (pre-arranged sparring form) of the shorei-kan karate teaching system (i.e., kiso kumite, bunkai kumite, etc.).

Part
III

Advanced
Techniques

Chapter 6

STANCES

Neko ashi dachi (cat stance)

1. The rear foot is on line AB at a 45-degree angle.
2. The front foot is on line AC. The distance between the heel of the rear foot and the toes of the front foot is two *sokucho* (foot length).
3. Only the ball of the front foot touches the ground but it has no weight on it.
4. Pull back the buttocks corresponding to the rear foot on an angle in order to protect the groin.
5. The shin of the front foot is perpendicular to the floor and the front leg's thigh is on a 45-degree angle to the floor.

Front view

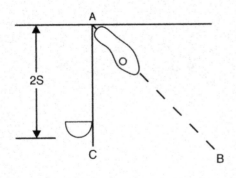

Stance basics:
(See diagrams AA and BB.)

Side view

(diagram AA)

ENBUSEN DIAGRAM

This diagram shows enbusen lines or the direction of kata. Kata, performed in these line directions only, begin at the center of the circle which is called the kiten. Stand here facing in the direction of enbusen line A (forward in the photographs). This position determines all others: to the student's back is B; to his right, C; to his left, D; and so forth.

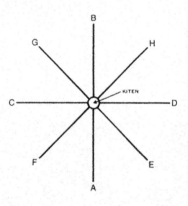

(diagram BB)

FOOT SCALE

Your foot length or sokucho determines stance measurements. One sokucho (1S) is one foot length, two sokucho (2S) are two foot lengths. The spot on the footmark indicates the ball of the foot (BF).

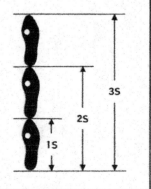

Forward:

A. Begin in neko ashi dachi.

B. Slide the front foot's heel forward keeping it on the ground.

C. Slide the rear foot forward and as it moves into the basic position bring the front foot's heel back off the ground with the ball of the foot maintaining contact (the front foot should have no weight on it).

Backward:

A. Begin in neko ashi dachi.

B. Put weight on the front foot (heel still off the ground) and immediately slide the rear foot backward.

C. Quickly draw back the front foot to the basic position.

(Key point: While moving forward or backward, keep the back straight and the hips drawn back.)

Chapter 7

STRIKES

Koken (bent wrist)

This strike is executed utilizing the apex of the bent wrist as the striking surface. It is very effective in a close-quarter fighting situation and is delivered in a quick snapping fashion. Main targets include the solar plexus, the floating ribs, the throat and the point just below the nose. The hand position is also used as an extremely effective goju-ryu blocking technique.

(Key point: With the wrist bent, the thumb, index and middle fingers should not touch each other.)

Kei koken ("the cock's beak" strike)

This strike utilizes the second knuckle of the index finger. The movement of the hand and wrist in this position resembles the striking motion of a fighting cock. The striking surface is quite small and thus concentrates tremendous force into a small area. This strike is very effective for striking a number of vital points on the body. These locations include the *suigetsu* (solar plexus), the *jinchu* (point just below the nose) and a point just under the *shinka* (heart), to name a few.

Chu koken

This strike uses the second knuckle of the middle finger. Although *chu koken* resembles *kei koken*, the essence of the strikes is different. Kei koken, by its nature, penetrates and attacks vital points. Chu koken is executed in a lateral movement with the wrist in a fixed position. The main targets are the temple and ribs. The technique is also used when you are on the ground to strike upward. In that case, use a circular motion of the arm to strike the groin area.

Hiraken

This strike utilizes the second knuckles of all four fingers, not including the thumb. (See illustration E.) It was designed to attack parts of the body which are impossible to reach effectively with a *seiken tsuki* (closed fist). For example, it would be difficult to deliver an effective strike to the throat with a seiken tsuki but devastating with a *hiraken*. This strike can easily crush the trachea and severely damage the throat.

(illustration E)

Chapter 8

BLOCKS

Ko uke (arc block)

1. The blocking point is on the wrist of the upper thumb side. (See illustration A.)

2. The first, second and third fingers should not touch each other. (See illustration A.)

3. The distance between the wrist and forehead is one-and-a-half feet in a 45-degree angle upward. (See illustration A.)

4. Head blocking hand always comes outside and chest palm-heel block comes inside. (Photos A-G)

5. Both hands move along the center line of the body. (Photos A-G)

Front View · A

(illustration A)

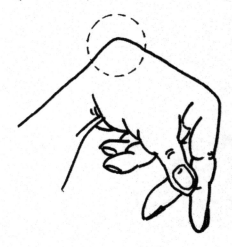

Side View · A

(continued on next page)

Front View D

E

Side View D

E

Hiki uke (hooking block)

1. The blocking point is on the outside of the wrist; bend the wrist outward. (See illustration B.)

2. The principle is the same as a regular chest block. (Refer to first volume of *Okinawan Goju-Ryu*)

Front View

A

(illustration B)

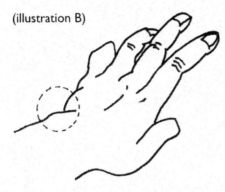

Side View

A

(continued on next page)

Front View D

E

Side View D

E

Gedan harai uke (low sweep block)

1. The principle of this block is the same as the regular closed-hand down block.
2. When finishing the block, push the palm heel downward. Fingers should be pointed toward you.

Front View · A

Side View · A

(continued on next page)

Front View D

E

Side View D

E

Ura uke (back-of-palm hooking block)

1. Bend wrist hard with palm heel out. (See illustration C.)

2. When finishing block, twist the forearm outward and snap the hand downward.

(illustration C)

(continued on next page)

Front View **D**

E

Side View **D**

E

Taihineri ko uke (body-twisting head arc block)

Key points:

1. Step back with right foot from an on-guard position into a zen stance, feet facing in direction C on enbusen diagram. (photo A-C)

2. Blocking hand first crosses in front of chest and upward at a 45-degree angle. (photo B)

3. Twist left shoulder back and twist left hip forward. (photo C)

4. Keep body straight and balanced. (photo C)

5. Block with forearm and maintain a 45-degree angle. (photo C)

Taihineri ura uke (body-twisting back-of-palm hooking block)

Key points:

1. Step back with right foot from an on-guard position into a zen stance, feet facing in direction C on enbusen diagram. (photo A-B)

2. Blocking hand first crosses in front of chest and upward at a 45-degree angle. (photo B)

3. Twist left shoulder back and twist left hip forward. (photo C)

4. Try not to raise blocking shoulder. (photo C)

5. Keep body straight and balanced. (photo C)

6. Block with outside forearm. (photo C)

Taihineri harai uke (body-twisting down block)

Key points:

1. Step back in the same manner as you did for a head block. (photo A-B)

2. Do a down block same as the gedan harai uke, except that you twist your body. (photo C)

3. Push the heel of your palm downward. (photo C)

Kuri uke (elbow block)

This block is executed by bringing the elbow downward to intercept the attack and protect the rib cage. It is designed to protect the side of the body and is executed in place while pivoting.

Sukui uke (upward scooping block)

This block is executed in neko ashi dachi and is designed against a *mae geri* (front kick). The technique employs a scooping motion to catch the attacking foot while having the groin (via neko ashi dachi) at a safe distance from the attacking foot.

Chapter 9

KICKS

Gedan sokuto geri ("foot sword")

In goju-ryu, this kick is principally aimed at the knees. The technique is executed in close proximity with a strong downward thrust and twist of the attacking foot. Distance to the opponent is proportional to the force that is exerted. The closer to the opponent, the more powerful the resultant kick. This technique does not produce the same potentially fatal results as does mae geri. Rather, it is designed to decisively incapacitate the opponent.

(photos on next page)

Front View  A

 B

Side View  A

 B

Part IV

Kata Gekiha
Dai Ichi
and
Bunkai

Chapter 10

KATA GEKIHA DAI ICHI

(Refer to diagram AA for enbusen lines.)

(diagram AA)

ENBUSEN DIAGRAM

This diagram shows enbusen lines or the direction of kata. Kata, performed in these line directions only, begin at the center of the circle which is called the kiten. Stand here facing in the direction of enbusen line A (forward in the photographs). This position determines all others: to the student's back is B; to his right, C; to his left, D; and so forth.

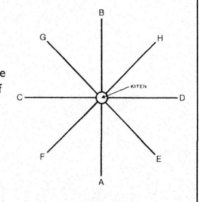

Attention and bowing.

Attention and ready position.

Open.

Double hands on guard;
right foot forward.

Pull left hand back slowly...

...and chest-punch fast.

Fast left chest block.
(Note: See gekisai #1 kata.)

Left foot steps forward as...

...right hand pulls back slowly...

...and delivers a fast chest punch.

Fast right chest block.

Right foot steps forward...

...and left hand pulls back slowly...

...then delivers a fast chest punch.

Fast left chest block.

Right foot steps back while executing
a left taihineri gedan harai uke.

Left foot steps back with a right taihineri harai uke.

Pivot fast while simultaneously executing a left taihineri ko uke facing direction C.

Step in direction C with a right chest punch.

Right foot steps back to direction D; execute a left down harai uke.

Left foot steps up to direction A with a right taihineri ko uke performed facing direction D.

Left foot steps into direction D while delivering a left chest punch.

Left foot steps back to direction C with a right down harai uke.

Left foot steps in direction A with a basic stance and deliver a left *mawashi hiki uke* (rotating hooking block).

Step forward with a right
mawashi hiki uke.

Left foot executes a mae geri.

Stomp and elbow attack. Open hands.

Left backfist.

Left down block.

Right undercut.

Right hand shuto uchi.

Left foot steps in direction B
with a left mawashi hiki uke.

Right foot steps in xvdirection B
with mawashi hiki uke.

Right foot steps back into a left
mawashi hiki uke.

Right foot readied for a kick.

Stomp and elbow attack.
Open both hands.

Right backfist.

Right down block.

Left undercut.

Left sweep chop to direction A.

Left foot slides back to direction B-C to cat stance simultaneously executing a right ura uke.

Slide up to direction A-D in a short zenkutsu dachi and perform a double-hand punch.

Right foot slides back to direction B-D in cat stance while simultaneously executing a left ura uke.

Slide up to direction A-C in a short zenkutsu dachi and perform a double-hand punch.

Left foot moves back to direction B in a cat stance and a right *tomoe uke* (circular block) is executed.

Close hands.   Ready.

Attention and bowing.

Chapter 11

GEKIHA DAI ICHI BUNKAI KUMITE

Attention.

Bowing.

Attention and ready.

Yoi (ready position).

Hirate (Open).

On guard.

(A) Step in and left chest punch.
(B) Step back and left chest block.

(B) In place. Right chest punch.
(A) In place. Left chest block.

(B) Step in and left chest punch.
(A) Step back and left chest block.

(A) In place. Right chest punch.
(B) In place. Left chest block.

(A) Step in and left chest punch.
(B) Step back and left chest block.

(B) In place. Right chest punch.
(A) In place. Left chest block.

(B) Step in at a 45-degree angle to shiko dachi and right down punch.
(A) Step back and right taihineri down block.

(B) Step in at a 45-degree angle to a shiko dachi and left down punch.
(A) Step back and left taihineri down block.

105

(B) Step in to basic stance and right head punch.
(A) Step back and right taihineri head block.

(A) Step in to basic stance and left chest punch.
(B) Steps back and left hiki uke.

(B) Steps in at 45-degree angle to shiko dachi and right down punch.
(A) Step back at 45-degree angle to shiko dachi and right down harai uke.

(A) Step in and left head punch.
(B) Steps back and left taihineri head block.

(B) Step in and right chest punch.
(A) Step back and right hiki uke.

(A) Step in at 45-degree angle into shiko dachi and left down punch.
(B) Step back at 45-degree angle to shiko dachi and left down block.

(B) Step in and right chest punch.
(A) Step back and right hiki uke.

(B) Step in and left chest punch.
(A) Step back with a left hiki uke.

(A) Prepare right foot for front kick.
(B) In place.

(A) Front kick.
(B) Slide back to right cat stance
and right sukui uke.

(A) Pull back.
(B) In place.

(A) Stamp and elbow attack to solar plexus.
(B) Slide right foot forward to left zenkutsu dachi and right shotei.

(A) Right backfist attack to chin.
(B) In place, push the elbow slightly.

(A) Right down block.
(B) Pivot to right zenkutsu dachi and left down punch.

(A) In place, left undercut.
(B) In place, right kuri uke.

(A) Right-hand sweep chop.
(B) In place, right head block.

(A) Step in and left chest punch.
(B) Step back and left hiki uke.

(B) Step in and right chest punch.
(A) Step back and right hiki uke.

(A) Step in and left chest punch.
(B) Step back and left hiki uke.

(A) In place.
(B) Prepare right foot for front kick.

(B) Front kick.
(A) Slide back to right cat stance
and right sukui uke.

(A) In place.
(B) Pull back kicking leg.

(B) Stamp and elbow attack to solar plexus.
(A) Right foot slide forward pivot to left, zenkutsu dachi and shotei.

(A) In place, push the elbow slightly.
(B) Right backfist attack to chin.

(A) Pivot to right zenkutsu dachi and left down punch.
(B) Right down block.

(B) In place, left undercut.
(A) In place, right kuri uke.

(B) Right-hand sweep chop.
(A) In place, right head block.

(A) Step in and left chest punch.
(B) Step back at 45-degree angle to cat stance and simultaneously left ura uke.

(B) Slide in and right chest punch.
(A) Slide back at 45-degree angle to cat stance and simultaneously right harai uke.

(A) Slide in with right foot forward and right chest punch.
(B) Slide back into right cat stance and simultaneously right ura uke.

(A) In place.
(B) Slide into short zenkutsu dachi and double punch.

(A) In place.
(B) Break A's side balance. *(Note: Grab the belt and push the shoulder.)* Then push A's side away.

On-guard in cat stance.

Close hands.

Ready. Bowing.

Attention.

Part
V

Ukemi
and
Kiso
Kumite
Dai Go

Chapter 12

UKEMI (BREAK FALL)

Key points:

1. When you fall, keep your head up and look at a 45-degree angle. Strike the floor with your hand open and never bend the elbow. The right foot and left hand hit the floor at the same time.

2. Pull the foot up to the groin area quickly to prepare for a kick.

3. After kicking, always pull the foot back quickly to the groin area, resuming the ready position.

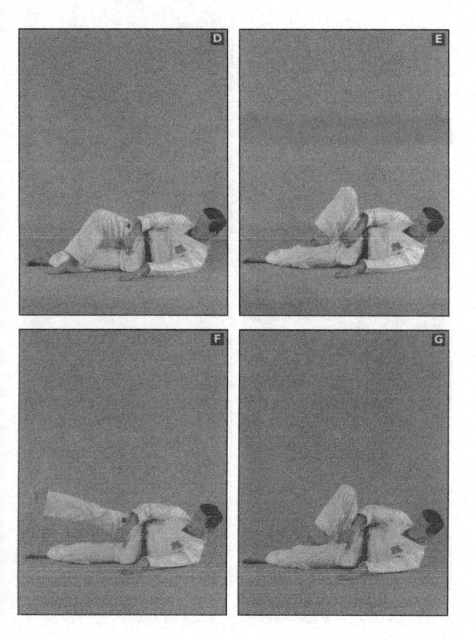

Chapter 13

KISO KUMITE DAI GO

(Sequence 1)°

On guard in a cat stance.

Slide in with a left head punch while defender moves back, executing a left ko uke.

Slide in with a right chest punch as opponent delivers a right hiki uke.

Move into a shiko dachi, striking with a left punch as defender slides back and executes a left harai uke.

Slide in with a right head punch. Opponent slides back into a cat stance with a right ko uke.

Sink back into a cat stance and execute a sukui uke against a right front kick.

Ready position in cat stances.

On guard in a cat stance.

Slide in with a left head punch while defender moves back, executing a left ko uke.

Slide in with a right chest punch as opponent delivers a right hiki uke.

Move into a shiko dachi, striking with a left punch as defender slides back and executes a left harai uke.

Slide in with a right chest punch. Opponent moves back with a right hiki uke.

Grab the right wrist and put your left forearm firmly on opponent's elbow while twisting your body left. *Caution: This can break the arm.* Then deliver a left, low side kick to the left knee.

On guard in a cat stance.

Slide in with a left head punch while defender moves back, executing a left ko uke.

Slide in with a right chest punch as opponent delivers a right hiki uke.

Move into a shiko dachi, striking with a left punch as defender slides back and executes a left harai uke.

Slide into a shiko dachi with a right
down punch. Opponent counters with a
right harai uke.

Right foot stamp in shiko dachi,
simultaneously performing a left
harai uke and right uppercut.

Kiso Kumite Dai Go (Sequence 4)

On guard in a cat stance.

Slide in with a left head punch while defender moves back, executing a left ko uke.

Slide in with a right chest punch as opponent delivers a right hiki uke.

Move into a shiko dachi, striking with a left punch as defender slides back and executes a left harai uke.

Slide in with a right chest punch. Defense is a
move back with a right hiki uke.

Push the right elbow with the left palm, simultaneously sliding the right foot into
into shiko dachi with a right *yoko empi* (sideways elbow strike).

On guard in a cat stance.

Slide in with a left head punch while defender moves back, executing a left ko uke.

Slide in with a right chest punch as opponent delivers a right hiki uke.

Move into a shiko dachi, striking with a left punch as defender slides back and executes a left harai uke.

Slide into shiko dachi with down block.

Grab the right wrist with left hand and right stomp into a shiko dachi...

...while at the same time thrusting right hand under the right thigh to throw opponent backward. While holding wrist, attack eyes with fingers while on the floor.

On guard in a cat stance.

Slide in with a left head punch while defender moves back, executing a left ko uke.

Slide in with a right chest punch as opponent delivers a right hiki uke.

Move into a shiko dachi, striking with a left punch as defender slides back and executes a left harai uke.

Slide in and right head punch.
Defense is a right ko uke.

Grab the right wrist with both hands and twist it downward,
simultaneously delivering a right foot step to the left and cross legs.

Then turn your body counterclockwise and pull the back left foot to right zenkutsu dachi while throwing a side hammer throw.

Pull the wrist up and down while delivering a right heel kick to the chest.

Part
VI

Koryu Kata Saifa and Its Bunkai Kumite

Chapter 14

KATA SAIFA

Kata saifa is one of the eight kaishu or ancient classical kata in Okinawan goju-ryu karate. Saifa is the first kaishu kata that is learned in shorei-kan. We do not know the meaning of the word "saifa" as Kanryo Higashionna never passed on this information. The kata is a compact one containing numerous techniques and fighting principles. By the application of kaisai no genri, we are able to discover the original techniques created and hidden by the ancient masters. Above all, classical kata should remain unchanged so that future generations may benefit from the knowledge contained within them.

Diagram AA (below) shows kihon enbusen: the directions a kata will travel. It should be referred to when studying any of the kata and many other movements and techniques from this book. The center of the diagram is called the kiten and it is where the kata begins.

The photos begin with Toguchi facing the direction A.

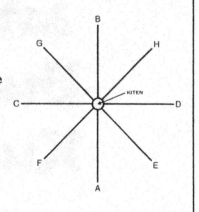

(diagram AA)

ENBUSEN DIAGRAM
This diagram shows enbusen lines or the direction of kata. Kata, performed in these line directions only, begin at the center of the circle which is called the kiten. Stand here facing in the direction of enbusen line A (forward in the photographs). This position determines all others: to the student's back is B; to his right, C; to his left, D; and so forth.

Attention.

Bow.

Attention.

Yoi.

Hirate.

Pull the right fist back with palm toward body and cover with left hand. Step right foot in direction F.

Slide the back foot up to *musubi dachi* (closed stance) while turning to direction D. Then execute a right *yoko hiji uchi* (sideways elbow strike).

The left foot slides back in direction B while looking in direction A into a shiko dachi. Then execute a left-hand *shotei otoshi uke* (downward block with palm heel) and then a right-hand *uraken otoshi uchi* (downward backfist strike).

Pull back left fist and cover with right palm. Look and step in direction E.

Slide the back foot up to musubi dachi while turning to direction C. Then execute a left yoko hiji uchi.

The right foot slides back in direction B while looking in direction A into shiko dachi. Then execute a right-hand shotei otoshi uke and then a left-hand uraken otoshi uchi.

Pull the right fist back with palm toward body and cover with left hand. Step right foot in direction F.

Slide the back foot up to musubi dachi while turning to direction D. Then execute a right yoko hiji uchi.

The left foot slides back in direction B while looking in direction A into shiko dachi. Then execute a left hand shotei otoshi uke and then a right hand uraken otoshi uchi.

Turn the head facing direction C while stepping the left foot to the right foot and then out in direction D. Then bring the right foot up to prepare for a mae geri and simultaneously execute a right hand harai uke and a left hand *mawashi sukui uke* (rotating upward palm block). Then turn head in direction A and execute a right leg mae geri. The hands do not move while executing the mae geri.

Turn the head facing direction D while sliding right foot in direction C and bringing the left foot to the right foot. Bring up the left foot to prepare for a mae geri and simultaneously execute a left hand harai uke and a right hand mawashi sukui uke. Then turn head in direction A and execute a left leg mae geri. The hands do not move while executing the mae geri.

After the mae geri, bring the left leg back into zenkutsu dachi. Execute a small left hand hiki uke and draw both hands back in preparation for a hiraken strike.

In place, execute a *morote hiraken tsuki*
(double fore-knuckle strike).

In place, circle both hands in front of the body and execute a right hand *kentsui uchi* (strike with side of closed fist) striking the open left hand. These hands meet at the center of the body at approximately belt level. While executing this technique, the body is bent forward at an angle that puts the left leg and the back in alignment. At the completion of this technique, the eyes are focused on the ground approximately five feet in front of the body.

Cross the right foot over while facing direction E in zenkutsu dachi and pivot to face direction B in the same stance. While turning, execute a left hand hiki uke.

In place, execute a morote hiraken tsuki.

In place, circle both hands in front of the body and execute a left-hand *kentsui uchi* (strike with side of closed fist) against the open right hand. These hands meet at the center of the body at approximately belt level. While executing this technique the body is bent forward at an angle which puts the right leg and the back in alignment. At the completion of this technique, the eyes are focused on the ground approximately five feet in front of the body.

Turn the head in direction A and execute a right foot *ashi barai* (upward foot sweep) and a *fumikomi* (foot stomp) in *hachiji dachi* (natural stance). At the same time, execute a left-hand shotei otoshi uke and a right-hand overhead kentsui uchi in direction A.

In place, facing the same direction, grab with the right hand and execute a left hand *soko tsuki* (undercut) while pulling the right hand back. At the same time, the left foot is pivoted on the ball of the foot parallel to the right foot.

Turn the head in direction B and execute a left-foot ashi barai and a fumikomi in hachiji dachi. At the same time, execute a right-hand shotei otoshi uke and a left-hand overhead kentsui uchi in direction B.

In place, (facing the same direction), grab with the left hand and execute a right-hand soko tsuki while pulling the left hand back to chamber. At the same time, the right foot is pivoted on the ball of the foot parallel to the left foot.

Step right foot in direction B in sanchin dachi and at the same time execute a right-hand *hari uke* (open-hand block with the palm facing upward) and immediately punch with a left-hand *chudan tsuki* (chest punch).

Step the left foot in direction B into zenkutsu dachi. Pivot on the left foot to the right to finish in neko ashi dachi with the right foot forward, facing direction A. Simultaneously execute a left-hand *chudan shotei osae uke* (lateral palm block) and then a right-hand *nai wan uchi* (strike using inside of forearm).

In place, execute a right-hand tomoe uke.

In place, bring the hands together as shown.

Bring the right foot back into musubi dachi and drop the hands into the yoi position.

Bring hands to sides and assume the *ki o tsuke* (attention) position.

Rei (bow) and finish.

Chapter 15

SAIFA
BUNKAI KUMITE

This subject, bunkai kumite, is an application of the classical kata, saifa. It is the first in a series of kumite for the goju-ryu classical kata. This bunkai illustrates and allows application of important principles of combat which are contained in goju-ryu kata.

Yoi.

(A) Right foot *suri ashi* (slide) and deliver a right-hand chudan tsuki.

(B) Do a left-foot backward suri ashi at a 30-degree angle into neko ashi dachi and block using shotei osae uke.

(B) Step right foot forward into shiko dachi and strike with the right *mae hiji uchi* (forward elbow strike).

(A) Move right foot back into shiko dachi and left-hand block using shotei osae uke.

(A) In place, perform a right-hand *gedan tsuki* (low punch).

(B) Slide the left foot up into sanchin dachi and with the base of the open left hand shotei otoshi uke with palm heel.

(B) In place, right-hand backfist to the jinchu. This strike is called *tate uraken uchi* (vertical backfist strike).

(A) In place, execute an open left *jodan ko uke* (high hand block).

(B) Right foot slides into sanchin dachi and a right-hand chudan tsuki is delivered.

(A) Left foot slides back at 30-degree angle into neko ashi dachi with a block using a *shotei osae uke* (lateral palm block).

(A) Step right foot forward into shiko dachi and strike with a right mae hiji uchi.

(B) Step right foot back into shiko dachi and block with a left shotei osae uke.

(B) In place, punch with a right gedan tsuki.

(A) Slide left foot up into sanchin dachi and execute a shotei otoshi uke with the left hand.

(A) In place, strike using a right tate uraken uchi to the jinchu.

(B) In place, execute a left jodan ko uke.

(A) Slide in with the right foot into sanchin dachi and deliver a right chudan tsuki.

(B) Slide back with the left foot at a 30-degree angle into neko ashi dachi and block using a left-hand shotei osae uke.

(B) Step right foot into shiko dachi and right-hand strike using a mae hiji uchi.

(A) Step right foot back into shiko dachi and left-hand block using shotei osae uke.

(A) In place, right-hand gedan tsuki.

(B) Slide left foot up into sanchin dachi and deliver a left shotei otoshi uke.

(B) In place, right-hand tate uraken uchi.

(A) In place, left-hand jodan ko uke.

(A) Step right foot forward into shiko dachi and throw a
right-hand gedan tsuki.

(B) Slide left foot back into neko ashi dachi and
right-hand gedan harai uke.

(B) In place, execute a right mae geri.

(A) Slide the right foot back into neko ashi dachi and
scoop the attacking foot with a sukui uke.

(B) Pull back to complete a mae geri.

(A) Hold position while kick is retracted.

(A) Slide the right foot into sanchin dachi and deliver a right-hand jodan tsuki.

(B) Slide right foot back into neko ashi dachi and execute a left-hand *jodan mawashi uke* (upper-level roundhouse block) by rotating the palm upward.

(A) In place, execute a left mae geri.

(B) Sink back into neko ashi dachi and deliver a right-hand sukui uke.

(B) Pull back to complete a mae geri.

(A) Hold position while kick is retracted.

(B) Step in with the left foot into zenkutsu dachi and double-strike with a morote hiraken tsuki.

(A) Step back into zenkutsu dachi with the right foot and double-block using hari uke.

(A) In place, pivot into a shiko dachi and punch with a left-hand gedan tsuki.

(B) In place, pivot into zenkutsu dachi and left-hand block using a *taihineri gedan harai uke* (body-twisting down block).

(B) In place, pivot into zenkutsu dachi and right-hand strike to the temple with a jodan kentsui uchi.

(A) In place, pivot into zenkutsu dachi and deliver a left-hand *taihineri jodan uke* (body-twisting head arc block).

(B) Step into sanchin dachi and strike with a right chudan tsuki.

(A) Step back with the left foot into sanchin dachi while delivering a right-hand *chudan uke* (mid-level block).

(A) Step into zenkutsu dachi with the left foot and strike with a morote hiraken tsuki.

(B) Step back with the right foot into zenkutsu dachi and block with a
morote hari uke (double open-hand block).

(A) In place, pivot into zenkutsu dachi and block with a left-hand taihineri gedan harai
uke. Then, while still in place, pivot to the left into zenkutsu dachi and strike the
temple with a right hand *jodan kentsui uchi* (upper-level strike with side of closed fist).

(B) In place, pivot into shiko dachi and execute a left gedan tsuki, then pivot to the
right into zenkutsu dachi and block with a left-hand taihineri jodan uke.

(A) In place, execute a left-hand chudan tsuki.

(B) Pivot into zenkutsu dachi and apply a right-hand shoei otoshi uke.

(A) In place, execute a right-hand jodan tsuki.

(B) In place, deliver a left-hand jodan uke.

(B) In place, circle the left arm while in contact with the punch in a counterclockwise direction and without stopping, continue the movement while pivoting to the right then immediately to the left and execute a left-hand kentsui uchi to the temple.

(A) In place, pivot into zenkutsu dachi and block with a left-hand taihineri jodan uke.

(Photo 28 and 29 techniques are done in one motion.)

(B) In place, strike with a right-hand soko tsuki.

(A) In place, deliver a left-hand kuri uke.

(B) In place, execute a left-hand chudan tsuki.

(A) In place, pivot into zenkutsu dachi with a right-hand shotei otoshi uke.

(B) In place, execute a right-hand jodan tsuki.

(A) In place, deliver a left-hand jodan uke.

(A) In place, circle the left arm while in contact with the punch in a counterclockwise direction and without stopping, continue the movement while pivoting to the right...

(B) In ready position for taihineri jodan uke.

(A) ...then immediately to the left and execute a left-hand kentsui uchi to the temple.

(B) Pivot to the right into zenkutsu dachi and apply a left-hand jodan uke.

(A) In place, throw a low, right-hand soko tsuki.

(B) In place, deliver a left-hand kuri uke.

(B) Slide right foot into sanchin dachi and execute a right-hand chudan tsuki.

(A) Slide back with the left foot into *renojii dachi* ("V" stance) and deliver a left-hand shotei osae uke.

(A) Slide in with the right foot forward into sanchin dachi stance
and execute a right chudan tsuki.

(B) Step left foot forward while simultaneously blocking with your left hand (shotei
osae uke) and lifting the right foot to prepare for gedan sokuto geri. At the same
time, the right arm is extended to deliver a nai wan uchi.

(B) Then strike with nai wan uchi and simultaneously deliver a gedan sokuto geri.

Naturally this combination of
techniques is…

…performed in rapid succession.

Glossary

ashi barai: upward foot sweep

bo: staff

bo dai ichi: staff kata number one (when "rhythm" is included, it indicates "performed to music")

bo dai ni: staff kata number two (when "rhythm" is included, it indicates "performed to music")

budo: martial way

bunkai: analysis of kata

bunkai kumite: two-person sequence of kata

bushi: highest term of respect for karateka

chishi: Chinese circular block-like tools with handles for strengthening wrists and forearms via swinging movements

chu koken: strike using second knuckle of middle finger

chudan shotei osae uke: lateral palm block (same as shotei osae uke)

chudan tsuki: chest punch

chudan uke: mid-level block

dan: black-belt rank

dohyo: sumo wrestling ring

dojo: training hall

enbusen: lines for performance of fight techniques

en-eki-ho: deductive method (see opposite: kino-ho)

fumikomi: foot stomp

gedan harai uke: low sweeping block

gedan tsuki: low punch

gedan uke: low block

gekiha: series of advanced kata

gekisai dai ichi: attack and smash number one

gekisai dai ni: attack and smash number two

goju-ryu: karate style blending hard and soft movements

hachiji dachi: natural stance

hakutsuru no mai: dance of a white crane; 10th hookyu kata performed to music

harai uke: sweeping block

hari uke: open-hand block with palm facing upward

hiki uke: hooking block

hiraken: strike using second knuckles of all four fingers

hirate: open

hojo undo: supplementary exercises including basic techniques and equipment

honbu: headquarters

hookyu kata: unified kata

hosoku joko: supplemental principles

hyomengi: apparent movements of fighting techniques

jinchu: point just below the nose

jiyu kumite: free sparring

jodan kentsui uchi: upper-level strike with side of closed fist

jodan ko uke: high hand block

jodan mawashi uke: upper-level roundhouse block

kaisai: applications hidden in koryu kata

kaisai no genri: theory on karate kata; guiding principle or theory of kaisai

kaisaigi: a technique found from a hyomengi through the work of kaisai

kaishu kata: pre-arranged sets of combative movements (consisting of basic punches) performed by one person; classical kata

kakidameshi: custom between karateka to test each other's fighting skills

kama: sickle that farmers in Okinawa converted to weapons

karateka: karate practitioner

kata: form

kata gekiha dai ichi: advanced kata number one

kei koken: strike using second knuckle of index finger; "the cock's beak" strike

kentsui uchi: strike with side of closed fist

ki: energy

ki o tsuke: command to "stand at attention"

kigu hjo undo: special equipment exercises to improve techniques and strength

kigu hojo undo: equipment exercises

kihon kata: basic kata: (sanchin, tenshu, naifanchi)

kino-ho: inductive method (see opposite: en-eki-ho)

kiso kumite: systematized pre-arranged sparring

kiso kumite dai go: systematized pre-arranged sparring number five

kiten: basic point

ko uke: arc block

kobo no jitsu: the essence of fighting

kobudo: weapons way

koken: bent wrist

kongoken: 100-pound oblong iron ring

koryu kata: classical form(s)

kumite: sparring

kumite renshu: sparring exercises

kuri uke: elbow block

kururunfa: one of eight koryu kata in goju-ryu; "forever peacefulness, stops, shatter" and/or "silence before the storm"

kyoshi: equivalent to eighth dan

mae geri: front kick

mae hiji uchi: forward elbow strike

makiwara: straw-padded striking post

matsubayashi-ryu: "pine forest style"; founded by Nagamine Shoshin

mawashi hiki uke: rotating hooking block

mawashi sukui uke: rotating upward palm block

morote hari uke: double open-hand block

morote hiraken tsuki: double fore-knuckle strike

musubi dachi: closed stance

naha-te: early traditional form of karate that later became goju-ryu

nai wan uchi: strike with inside of forearm

naifanchi: a family of three kata: naifanchi shodan, nidan and sandan; unique because they are the only kata that exclusively employ lateral movements

neko ashi dachi: cat stance

nunchaku: weapon made of two rods joined by short chain or rope

otoshi uke: base-of-palm block

rei: bow

renojii dachi: "V" stance

renshi: equivalent to seventh dan

roka: hallway or foyer

sai: fork-dagger featuring two curved prongs

saifa: one of eight koryu kata in goju-ryu; "smash and tear"

sanchin: "three battles"

sanchin dachi: basic "hourglass" stance

sanseiru: one of eight koryu kata in goju-ryu; "36 hands" (or "36 techniques")

sashi: stone or concrete blocks, usually used in pairs for exercise; "thrusting stones"

seiken tsuki: closed fist

seipai: one of eight koryu kata in goju-ryu; "18 hands" (or "18 techniques")

seisan: one of eight koryu kata in goju-ryu; "13 hands" (or "13 techniques")

sempai: senior

sensei: teacher

seyunchin: one of eight koryu kata in goju-ryu; "pull into battle" and/or "conquer over distance"

shamisen: guitar-like string instrument

shihan: master teacher

shiko dachi: square stance where feet are turned at 45-degree angles

shinka: heart

shisochin: one of eight koryu kata in goju-ryu; "conquer in four directions"

shorei-kan: school of goju-ryu founded by Toguchi after death of his teacher, Chojun Miyagi (founder of goju-ryu)

shorin-ryu: "small forest style," "young forest style" and/or "pine forest style"

shotei: palm heel

shotei osae uke: lateral palm block (same as chudan shotei osae uke)

shotei otoshi uke: downward block with palm heel

shuto uchi: knife-hand strike

shuyo san gensuko: three main principles

soko tsuki: undercut

sokucho: foot length

suigetsu: solar plexus

sukui uke: upward scooping block against a kick

sumo: Japanese wrestling

suparinpei: one of eight koryu kata in goju-ryu; "108 hands" (or "108 techniques")

suri ashi: slide

taihineri gedan harai uke: body-twisting down block (same as taihineri harai uke)

taihineri harai uke: body-twisting down block (same as taihineri gedan harai uke)

taihineri jodan uke: body-twisting head arc block (same as taihineri ko uke)

taihineri ko uke: body-twisting head arc block (same as taihineri jodan uke)

taihineri ura uke: body-twisting back-of-palm hooking block

tanden: abdomen

tate uraken uchi: vertical backfist strike

te: empty-hand fighting acts (literally translates as "hand")

tensho: "revolving hands"

toki to musubi: original term for "kaisai"

toki to musubi no genri: original term for "kaisai no genri"

Tomari-te: literally "Tomari hand"; one of three original Okinawan karate styles

tomoe uke: circular block

tonfa: old farming tool developed as a weapon by Okinawan farmers

ukemi: breakfalls; *methods of* safely falling or receiving techniques

unsoku: footsteps

ura uke: back-of-palm hooking block

uraken otoshi uchi: downward backfist strike

yakusoku kumite: pre-arranged sparring form

yakuza: gangster

yobi undo: series of warm-up exercises

yoi: command to "get ready"; ready position

yoko empi: sideways elbow strike

yoko hiji uchi: sideways elbow strike (same as "yoko empi")

zenkutsu dachi: long stance with front knee bent

DOMESTIC VIOLENCE

Tragedy and Hope

Frances T. Pilch (ed)

with Howard Black, Janet Kerr, Patricia L. Lostroh, Dave McCone, Douglas Miles, and Erika Vida

Robert D. Reed Publishers

Robert D. Reed Publishers • Bandon, OR

Robert D. Reed Publishers
P.O. Box 1992
Bandon, OR 97411
Phone: 541-347-9882; Fax: -9883
E-mail: 4bobreed@msn.com
Website: www.rdrpublishers.com

Editor: Cleone Reed
Designer: Amy Cole
Front Cover Art: Jane Sterrett
Cover: Cleone Reed
Author photo: Jay Billups Creative Media

Soft Cover ISBN: 978-1-944297-92-3
EBook ISBN: 978-1-944297-93-0

Library of Congress Control Number: 2021930538

Designed and Formatted in the United States of America

DEDICATION

To all those who struggle
to find their way out of the
abyss of domestic violence
and to those who seek
to help them

Contents

ACKNOWLEDGMENTS

The contributors to this book, *Domestic Violence: Tragedy and Hope*, would like to express gratitude to their families and friends for their encouragement and support. In addition, we commend Robert D. Reed Publishers for their openness to publishing important new books on critical social issues. Cleone Reed has been deeply invested in our project and has provided expert advice on formatting and editing. Amy Cole has been instrumental in the design of our book. Jane Sterrett contributed the art and design for the front cover. Her work is incredibly creative and unique, and her generosity is unparalleled. Amanda Udis-Kessler gave her enthusiastic permission for us to include the lyrics to one of her musical pieces, "Love Her Before You Judge Her." Dave McCone conducted essential and insightful interviews of Howard Black and Doug Miles.

A huge thank you to those who read and endorsed this book! We hope that all those involved in the effort to aid victims and find solutions to this devastating problem will find our book helpful as they continue their challenging work. Finally, our hearts go out to victims everywhere who have suffered abuse at the hands of an intimate partner.

Love Her Before You Judge Her

It's midnight. She calls you. She just needs a friend.
She says it's her husband. He hit her again.
She's frightened. She loves him. She can't understand.
He's gentle, then crazy. It gets out of hand.
You tell her to leave him. She says there's no way.
You hang up the phone. How can she stay?

Love her before you judge her. See her point of view.
She is trapped by dreams she had and nightmares coming true.
Caring is mixed with terror and shame is mixed with pride.
Love her before you judge her. Listen and take her side.

He handles the money. The car's in his name.
He tells her he loves her, then says she's to blame.
He swears that he's changing if she'd just believe.
He swears that he'll kill her if she tries to leave.
Would he hurt their daughter? There's no way to know.
With all that's at stake how can she go?

Love her before you judge her. Walk inside her shoes.
Everything she has right now is something she could lose.
Leaving will bring more danger than choosing to remain.
Love her before you judge her. She never chose this pain.

It's midnight. She's frightened. She calls 911.
He says she'll be sorry for all that she's done.
These calls are a nuisance. The cop's not impressed.
"Domestic disturbance." He makes no arrest.
The cop leaves. He hits her. The call did no good.
How foolish she was to think it would.

Love her before you judge her. Work to save her life.
Build a world that won't dismiss her simply as his wife.
If we restore her power, we give her back her choice,
Trusting in her decisions and honoring her voice,
Holding the ones who cause the harm accountable instead.
Loving instead of judging, mending the broken thread.

Music and Lyrics by Amanda Udis-Kessler

CONTRIBUTORS

Howard Black is currently the Director of Communications and Public Information Officer in the Office of the District Attorney, 4th Judicial District, Colorado. His law enforcement career began in 1978 and includes over 40 years of experience with the Colorado Springs Police Department (CSPD) and the El Paso County Sheriff's Office (EPSO). During that time he managed the Special Victims Section of the Investigations Division. His Section had responsibility for the Adult Sexual Assault Unit, Domestic Violence Unit, Crimes Against Elders Unit, Forensic Interview Unit, Forensic Sketch Artist Unit, Registered Sex Offender Unit, Runaway Unit, and two Crimes Against Children Units. He co-managed CSPD's Domestic Violence Federal Grant. Howard has served on advisory panels for the International Association of Chiefs of Police (Identifying and Promoting the Adoption of Innovative Strategies to Reduce Domestic Violence Incidents Involving Police Officers) and the Police Executive Research Forum (Police Responding to Violence Against Women).

Janet L. Kerr, MA, LPC, has worked for the prevention of Domestic and Sexual Violence since 1986. Ms. Kerr is a psychotherapist and consultant providing training and technical assistance to professionals nationally and internationally about issues related to Domestic and Sexual Violence. Prior to her work as a consultant, Ms. Kerr served as the Executive Director of TESSA in Colorado Springs. She is an adjudicated expert providing testimony in domestic violence court cases throughout Colorado and in Military Courts.

Patricia L. Lostroh has been the Executive Director of Genesis House since 2000. Genesis House, located in David City, Nebraska, is a support center for victims of Domestic Violence that offers a long term transitional program of mentoring and practical assistance as well as domestic violence prevention education. Previously she served as a Victim Assistance Director with law enforcement (1994–2013).

Dave McCone is a Professor of Psychology at the US Air Force Academy where he studies sexual assault prevention. He gained perspective on domestic violence issues while serving on the Board of Directors for TESSA, an agency in southern Colorado that provides services and education for domestic violence survivors and the surrounding community. Dr. McCone earned a PhD in Clinical Child Psychology from the University of Oregon. Prior to joining the faculty at the US Air Force Academy he was on staff at the University of Utah Neuropsychiatric Institute in Salt Lake City.

Douglas J Miles is a County Court Judge in Colorado Springs, Colorado. Judge Miles has over thirty years' experience in the domestic violence field as a prosecutor, consultant, trainer, and judicial officer. He is currently the presiding judge of the Domestic Violence Court, a problem-solving court for repeat misdemeanor and felony DV offenders.

Frances T. Pilch is Professor Emeritus of Political Science at the United States Air Force Academy. Her areas of expertise include genocide and violence against women. She was awarded a Fulbright to Mongolia and a Fulbright-Hays to South Africa, and was named the Colorado Professor of the Year in 2011–12.

Erika Vida started as a first responder volunteer with Colorado Springs PD and found her passion for working with survivors of Violent Crime in 2012. She was awarded her MS in Criminal Justice with an emphasis in Security in Policing in 2015. Erika is currently the Program Coordinator for the Teller County Victim Assistant Program, and is committed to providing trauma-informed resources and supportive services to the community.

INTRODUCTION

As this book is being written, we are in the middle of a pandemic: Covid-19. But there is another pandemic raging in our community, in the United States, and around the world – domestic violence (DV). Violence against women and violence in intimate relationships exist everywhere. Although some strides have been made in dealing more openly with DV, it is debatable as to whether the problem has diminished. Many experts maintain that it not only has not gone away, it is as pervasive as ever. And it will persist long after the coronavirus pandemic has ended.

Domestic violence is exacerbated by isolation of the victim. Predictably, the isolation of families caused by Covid-19 has served to greatly increase the incidence of domestic violence and abuse. It has become very difficult for victims to cry out for help when their abusers are in close proximity so much of the time and when contact with the outside world is so curtailed. Communities are finding that when restrictions are lifted, the need for interventions and services for victims is huge. We are facing a problem of gigantic proportions, and one that is incredibly complex and difficult to address. Yet it is incumbent upon us to try to find answers to a problem that has plagued humanity for generations.

This book is unique in its construction and vision. After a brief introduction to the extent of the domestic violence problem in our community and beyond, the reader will be presented with "Suzanne's Story." This is a fictional account of a woman named Suzanne, whose relationship with Rob, who becomes her husband, descends incrementally into a cycle of abuse and violence. Her story was created by one of the contributors, Janet Kerr, who has extensive experience with victims of domestic violence. She has woven together fragments from hundreds of cases with which she has worked, to paint a picture of the many elements that contribute to situations in which domestic violence and abuse prevail. The reader is asked to follow Suzanne on her journey into a dangerous and damaging relationship.

Following "Suzanne's Story" are commentaries on the psychology of DV and perspectives provided by law enforcement, a victim advocate, and a judge (and former District Attorney). These unique perspectives give us insight into the system surrounding a victim. The law enforcement commentary provides us with understanding as to how a cop might think about DV and experience DV calls. The functioning of the judicial system is explained as it applies to DV. The victim advocate talks about her role in seeking safety for victims, and a short description of potential community resources is provided. The book concludes with "the rest of the story," featuring thoughts from our law enforcement representative, observations from a community leader who has worked with hundreds of DV victims, and finally, the perspective of a DV survivor on Suzanne's Story.

Although abusers and victims can be both women and men, the book employs "he/him" for abusers, for simplicity's sake, because the majority of DV perpetrators tend to be male. This is not to say, however, that females are never perpetrators. Abuse exists in all kinds of relationships. Nevertheless, many of the characteristics of these power and control situations are the same.

The goal of the book is to provide the reader with a better understanding of the complexity of DV issues. There are no simple answers; there are no easy solutions. However, there is a deeply held cultural bias against victims. Whether we like it or not, many observers will blame victims for getting into bad relationships in the first place, or staying in them once it is clear that they are damaging and dangerous. This book seeks to show the reader how insidious the process of disempowering and controlling a victim can be, and how hard it is to break cycles of control and abuse. If we have opened at least a few eyes to the complexities of DV, we have done what we set out to do.

The contributors, with one exception, are all from Colorado Springs, and their personal experiences and perspectives are drawn from this community. The perspective of a community leader from

Nebraska is included to demonstrate the tragic universality of domestic violence. Domestic violence is ubiquitous. It is everywhere – both at home in the United States and abroad. It affects the rich and the poor, the educated and the non-educated, all racial groups and ethnic communities, and persons of all religious persuasions. The tactics used by abusers to attain and assert power and control over their victims are remarkably similar the world over – isolation, disempowerment, crippling of self-esteem, and fear. Therefore, one should not view this book as relating only to Colorado Springs. Hopefully the messages and information in these pages will enlighten people everywhere.

"The effects of abuse are devastating and far-reaching. Domestic violence speaks many languages, has many colors, and lives in many different communities."

— Sandra Pupatello

1

Domestic Violence: The Magnitude of the Problem

Frances T. Pilch

In 2018, our community was rocked by a horrendous case involving domestic/intimate partner violence. Kelsey Berreth, 29 years old, was killed by her boyfriend, Patrick Frazee, in Woodland Park, CO. Kelsey was bludgeoned to death; their toddler daughter was in the same room when it happened. Earlier that year, in Frederick, Colorado, which is about 90 miles from Colorado Springs, Shanann Watts, 34 years old, was killed by her husband. Shanann was pregnant with their third child. Christopher Watts also killed his two young daughters. And these cases, that received widespread national attention, are just the tip of the iceberg. Many cases in marginalized communities do not receive the attention that they deserve.

Tragically, violence against women or intimate partner violence is rampant not only in our community but throughout the world. I remember one time when I was in a room full of eleven women in a township in Johannesburg, South Africa. The women ranged in ages from about 20 to 73. As we started to talk about our lives and dreams, one of the ladies, a beautiful young teacher, mentioned that she had almost died as a result of an attack by her husband. I asked the group how many of them had experienced domestic violence – not just verbal or emotional abuse, but physical violence. Astonishingly, every single one of those women had suffered physical violence at the hands of an intimate partner or family member.

In Mongolia, as I looked out a bus window, I personally witnessed a man beating a woman on the street. Alcohol is a huge problem in Mongolia, and domestic violence is often related to excessive alcohol use. In India, I knew a family where the youngest daughter was married off to a wealthy man. She was in the "untouchable" caste, and she was very beautiful. Within six months she had been returned, beaten to a pulp, because she had not "adequately pleased her husband."

Millions of women around the world are killed or abused every year by their partners. The situation has only been made worse by the coronavirus pandemic. Economic hardship and isolation have affected families everywhere, putting tremendous stress on relationships and causing calls to hotlines to increase by as much as 75% in countries around the world. In some areas the calls have NOT increased – and that is a cause for concern as well. It might indicate that reaching out for help is impossible for victims when their abusers are always present.

The problem of violence against women is truly a worldwide pandemic, fueled by cultural ideas about the "proper" role of women as subservient to men – in marriage and in life. Recognizing the magnitude of the problem of domestic violence is the first step towards finding ways to address it.

In the United States, more than 10 million adults experience domestic violence (DV)/Intimate Partner Violence (IPV) annually. This violence can take various forms – physical, emotional, sexual, and/or psychological. People of all cultures, genders, sexual orientations, socioeconomic status, races, and religions experience IPV. About a third of all female murder victims in the US are killed by an intimate partner. From 2016 through 2018 the number of intimate partner violence victimizations in the US increased by 42%.[1] The magnitude of the problem is astonishing. "One in four women and one in ten men experience sexual violence, physical violence, and/or stalking by an intimate partner during their lifetime with "IPV-related impact," such as being concerned for their safety, PTSD symptoms, injury, or needing victim services. Approximately one in five female victims and one in twenty male victims need medical care."[2]

The Colorado Domestic Violence Fatality Review Board was established in 2017 by the Colorado General Assembly. The board includes the Attorney General or his or her designee, who acts as chair, and at least 17 other members, appointed by the Attorney General. The board is mandated to coordinate with local and regional domestic violence review teams to collect data, to review and analyze the data, and to prepare recommendations for the General Assembly. It is required to submit annual reports by December 1 through December 2021.

Colorado Attorney General Phil Weiser noted, "The work of the Domestic Violence Fatality Review Board is critical to our state's overall strategy to understand domestic violence and prevent fatalities and near-death incidents. The findings in this report can and should be integrated into our state's policies around domestic violence response and prevention. We owe it to the victims and survivors to find effective methods to prevent these tragedies in Colorado."[3]

According to its 2018 report, domestic violence deaths in Colorado increased significantly from 2017.[4] Of those killed in 2018, the youngest was 3 and the oldest was 64. 47% of the victims were women killed by a current or former male partner. Gunshot violence was the most common form of death (63%). Perpetrators had a history of domestic violence in 72.7% of the cases. Four of the findings in this

---

[1] R.E. Morgan and B.A. Oudekerk, "Criminal Victimization, 2018." Bureau of Justice Statistics.
[2] National Coalition Against Domestic Violence, Fact Sheet on Domestic Violence. Available online at ncadv.org.
[3] Available online at https://coag.gov/press-releases/12-12-19.
[4] Kieran Nicholson, "Domestic Violence Deaths in Colorado Increased in 2018." *Denver Post*, December 13, 2019.

report are especially interesting: "More than 80% of the perpetrators had a history of drug or alcohol abuse; more than 80% of the perpetrators exhibited possessiveness of the victim; more than 90% of the perpetrators had a significant loss of perceived control, and more than 90% of perpetrators were experiencing feelings of abandonment or betrayal."[5] Local review boards, like the Denver Domestic Violence Fatality Review Board, assist in the collection of data and information. However, their ability to do so is sometimes constrained by lack of resources.

Between 2013 and 2016, 100 Colorado women were killed by a current or former intimate partner. According to a fact sheet produced by the National Coalition Against Domestic Violence, 36.8% of Colorado women and 30.5% of Colorado men experience intimate partner physical violence, intimate partner sexual violence, and or intimate partner stalking in their lives. A 2019 survey of 88% of Colorado domestic violence programs found that on the day of the survey, participating programs reported serving 1,221 adults and children; on that same day, 269 needs were unmet due to lack of resources. As of December 31, 2019, Colorado had submitted 419 domestic violence misdemeanor and 330 active protective order records to the NICS Index. On a typical day, local domestic violence hotlines receive an average of 13 calls every minute.

In Colorado, domestic violence misdemeanants are prohibited from possessing firearms. This prohibition does not apply to dating abusers. Respondents to final and ex parte protective orders are prohibited from possessing firearms for the duration of the order.

According to TESSA, the nonprofit that serves to assist victims of domestic violence and sexual assault in El Paso and Teller counties, approximately 45 calls about DV are made daily to the police. The other day I noted the police blotter in my small community

---

[5] These facts were based on the findings of the Colorado Domestic Violence Fatality Review Board Report, released in 2019.

newspaper. This area includes only two zip codes. In one week, there had been 24 police reports. Of these, 12 were for "domestic violence." Astonishing! This translates to more than 16,000 DV police calls a year. And so many DV incidents are never reported at all!

The Colorado Springs community is unique in that several military installations are located nearby – to include Peterson Air Force Base, Fort Carson Army Base, and the United States Air Force Academy. Military families can be impacted by DV, especially when partners return from deployments. While the military deals with DV that takes place on its bases, if families live off base the realities of DV situations must be addressed by the Colorado Springs Police Department. Cooperation between the military and the City of Colorado Springs on these matters has been absolutely necessary.

How do we define domestic violence? "Domestic violence is the willful intimidation, physical assault, battery, sexual assault, and/ or other abusive behavior as part of a systematic pattern of power and control perpetrated by one intimate partner against another. It includes physical violence, sexual violence, threats, economic, and emotional/psychological abuse."[6]

The scope of the problem of domestic violence is horrifying. The human toll it takes is tragic. It can prove to be extremely lethal, particularly when a victim tries to leave her relationship with her abuser. It is devastating to children. What follows is "Suzanne's Story," a fictional account constructed to demonstrate the way an abusive relationship can develop and the difficulties in leaving such a relationship. We hope that you will read it, analyze it, and come away with a more nuanced understanding of the complexities of DV situations, including the constellation of instruments and agents that seek to intervene and assist victims.

---

[6] National Coalition Against Domestic Violence Fact Sheet, op. cit.

15

"*I did not know that the first step in any domestic violence relationship is to seduce and charm the victim. I also did not know that the second step is to isolate the victim. The next step in the domestic violence pattern is to introduce the threat of violence and see how she reacts. We victims know something you [non-victims] usually don't. It's incredibly dangerous to leave an abuser because the final step in the domestic violence pattern is to 'kill her'. Over 70% of domestic violence murders happen after the victim has ended the relationship.*"

— Leslie Morgan Steiner

Suzanne's Story

Janet Kerr

Rob and I fell in love fast. At the time, it felt like a classic whirl-wind romance complete with flowers and surprise outings. I was working in a coffee shop, putting myself through school, and he came in every morning on his way to work to get his customary grande macchiato. Although I had sworn off relationships, a month after our first outing (it was not a date, I insisted to Rob) we were spending nearly every night together.

Rob had recently gotten out of a three-year off-and-on relationship with Amanda, a woman he met online. He swore he would never use another dating site, talking about how it's too easy to pretend you are someone you're not. Amanda, it seems, was crazy. According to Rob, she was jealous, controlling, and manipulative. I could sympathize. I knew the type. I myself had broken up with the guy I dated throughout my freshman and sophomore years a few months earlier. I stayed with Jason longer than I wanted because every time I tried to end it, he freaked out. He'd blow up my phone, follow me from class proclaiming his undying love, plead with my friends and family to talk to me on his behalf, and twice he actually threatened to commit suicide if I left.

After the Jason fiasco, I was reconnecting with friends I had neglected. It was so refreshing to have my freedom back, not that I had a lot of down time between school and work. Even though I was not ready for anything serious, I didn't want to risk losing Rob. Being courted, being romanced felt amazing. No one had ever treated me so well. My friends were soon protesting that they had fallen off my radar again. I made plans with them and told Rob that the coming Friday night was girls' night. He looked crest-fallen but told me I should go. The next morning when he came into the coffee shop, he presented me with concert tickets for one of my favorite bands. Unfortunately, the concert was on Friday. He said he had bought them a week before as a surprise, and that was why he was so disappointed when I told him I had made other plans. Of course, I couldn't let him think I didn't appreciate his thoughtful gesture. Girls' night could be rescheduled. On Friday night I noticed the purchase date on the tickets was actually the same day that I told Rob about girls' night, not a week earlier as he had claimed, and I was irritated. He'd lied to me. I took a deep breath and decided that if he had gone to the trouble and expense of getting the tickets, I should let my irritation go. I am glad I let it go because we had a great time at the concert.

Our sex life was incredible, mostly. Rob liked to push the boundaries, never too far, just a little beyond my comfort zone. It was edgy and exciting. I sometimes found myself wanting more love making, but he always remarked about how sexy I was, and how he could not resist my "sweet little ass." We unfailingly got caught up in the intensity of the moment.

We all know what can come from unplanned, impromptu sex … babies. We discussed all the options when I got pregnant. It is probably more accurate to say that I tried to discuss all the options. Rob really pushed to get married. Truthfully, I wasn't ready to be a mother. I was 21 years old. We had only been together for four months. My initial inclination was to terminate the pregnancy or adopt out. My mom and my friends urged me not to get married, which really upset Rob. The intensity of Rob's belief in us was so strong, I got swept up. I also got swept up in guilt. He peppered me with questions: Didn't I love him? Didn't I want to have his child? Didn't I believe in him and his commitment to take good care of us? He was seven years older and had a good job at an accounting firm. I reasoned that I did indeed love him and would end up marrying him at some point, so why not just do it now?

The wedding was small. Rob wanted the two of us to slip off to the courthouse. He said he didn't want anyone at the wedding who wasn't 100% behind us. Fortunately, after lots of talking, I was able to convince him that everyone's concerns were not about us as a couple or him as a man, but simply about our circumstances. I fibbed about that a little. My mom and friends expressed concern that Rob seemed to be pressuring me, but I assured them this was what I wanted.

We got married June 1, right after I finished my semester. My original plan was to take two summer classes, but Rob urged me to take the summer off, which I was happy to do because I was really sick. I wish it was "morning sickness." I threw up throughout the day and evening for four-and-a-half months. The plan was for me to return to school in the fall but take off the winter semester as the baby was due in February. I made it clear to Rob that finishing my degree was a priority. Mom always encouraged me to go to college. She never had the opportunity, and she emphasized the importance of not being dependent on anyone.

Although my father was a reliable bread winner, he wasn't very trustworthy in other ways. In fact, he made our lives miserable. I remember disappearing under my covers with a book and a flashlight when Dad came home "in a mood." That is what my mother called it. She would say, "Your father is in a mood, Suzanne. Let's give him time to wind down." Translation: be quiet, make sure your room is picked up, don't cause a fuss. I would head to my bed, stopping in the bathroom first to make sure there was no toothpaste in the sink. Dad was particular about a lot of things, but he especially could not abide toothpaste in the sink.

Being invisible was the best way to avoid Dad's wrath. I slept on the floor in a sleeping bag that I folded every morning and stowed under my bed because I could rarely make my bed tight and smooth enough to meet his standard. When I was nine, I thought I found a way to cut myself off from him even more. I put on headphones to block out his shouting, but I soon learned that was a bad idea. If he was yelling for me and I didn't respond, there was hell to pay.

It was mid-summer, time for me to choose classes for fall semester. Rob saw me looking at the online catalog. "Do you really want to go back?" he asked. "You're still not feeling great, you keep changing your mind about your major, and you've already racked up a shit-load of student debt. With the baby coming, you won't go to work anytime soon. Does it really make sense right now?"

I replied, "You know how important a degree is to me, and I 'don't keep changing my mind.' I've switched once from Sociology to Early Childhood Education so I can get a teaching certificate. We've already agreed that it would be great if I could teach so I could have summers and breaks with the kids."

"Why settle for summers when you can be at home full-time? Besides, I'll already be paying off your loans for years! On a teacher's salary, it'll take forever to for you break even," Rob argued. He seemed to be getting a little spun-up, so I closed the computer and asked him what he wanted for dinner. He loved my cooking and it was something I took pride in.

To say Mom was not happy when I told her I didn't think I would return to school was an understatement. She always regretted not getting a degree. After one especially nasty episode with Dad, I suggested to her that we leave. Her response was disappointing but understandable: "How? With what? Life is expensive – rent, food, insurance, utilities, car, gas, clothes – the list goes on and on. He would never pay maintenance or child support – he told me as much. He'd keep me tied up in court for years. And I certainly don't have money for an attorney." Now she was telling me not to fall into the same trap. I was incensed. How could she compare my situation with hers? Rob was nothing like my cruel father. I leapt to his defense.

The first time Rob lost his temper with me, I was shocked. It seemed so unlike him. It was such a little thing. We were on our way to the movies when I realized I had forgotten my glasses. "How could you be so stupid," he said with a tone of contempt reminiscent of my father. Pregnancy hormones were running rampant and I burst into tears. Then he accused, "You are just like Amanda, that manipulative cunt." I sat in stunned silence as we drove back to the house. When he pulled into the driveway and told me in an irritated voice to "hurry up," I realized we were still going to the movies.

I returned to the car, glasses in hand and apologized, explaining that pregnancy brain was making me forgetful and emotional. "I wasn't trying to manipulate you," I implored. He reached out for my hand and I was so relieved. In the theater, he came back from the refreshment stand with our standard popcorn and drink order, plus a giant box of Milk Duds, my favorite movie candy. That was his way of apologizing. He really could be wonderfully attentive and thoughtful.

When the ultrasound revealed that we were having a girl, I could tell Rob was disappointed, even though he did not say anything. His general enthusiasm for all things baby related just evaporated. He gave me a decorating budget that was significantly smaller than our original discussions. When I asked for his opinion about paint color or a theme, he said he was fine with whatever as long as it was within budget.

The holidays were not the warm, joyous season I had imagined. I wanted us to start our own traditions full of family and friends, but everything I suggested or did irritated him. One of the few happy memories of my father was of the family going together to cut down a tree the Saturday after Thanksgiving. When I suggested we do the same, it was met with derision. "Paying for a real tree every year is a waste. We'll get an artificial one after Christmas when they go on sale."

Rob loves sugar cookies so I invited Mom over to help me make a big batch. We had so much fun decorating cookies, though the attempt was quite amateurish. Still, they tasted delicious. When Rob got home, he didn't even bother to try one because he said they looked like a three-year-old had made them. "Your loss," my mom said cheerfully as she popped a cookie into her mouth. He did not speak to her the rest of the evening. I felt relieved when she left, but unfortunately the tension remained. "What's wrong?" I asked Rob.

"I don't appreciate your mother's sass!" Rob declared.

"Sass?" I wondered, truly confused.

"How dare she come into my home and speak to me like that! 'Your loss,'" he mocked. As I tried to explain that Mom wasn't being disrespectful, that in fact he was the one who had been a jerk with his nasty attitude, he became enraged. He threw the platter of cookies into the kitchen wall. "Clean that up, bitch!" he roared as he grabbed his keys and left the house.

I sobbed as I cleaned the mishmash of cookies, frosting, sprinkles, and platter. I could not, would not do this – I would not raise my daughter with an unpredictable father who intermittently terrorized us. But where to go? I had talked Rob up so often to my mom and friends (always trying to downplay their concerns), I felt stupid going to them with this story. A motel? That was not in Rob's budget, but I had squirreled away some money to surprise Rob with a beer club membership for Christmas. Mom had agreed to charge the membership on her credit card and I would reimburse her in cash. I found a cheap motel room online, packed a change of clothes, and left.

At 1 AM my phone blew up with texts and calls from Rob. I turned off the ringer and put the phone in a drawer, but I couldn't sleep. I checked the phone at 4:00. Rob was asking if the baby was okay. Was I at the hospital? I texted back to let Rob know I was fine and we could talk in the morning. Still unable to sleep, I headed home at 6 AM.

Rob was frantic and full of regret, "Suzanne, I am so sorry."

"You scared the hell out of me," I said.

He replied, "That is the last thing I want to do. You scared me too. I was afraid you weren't coming back." He truly seemed despondent at the thought of me leaving, and I remembered the stories he told me from his childhood about his mom. He described her as a "me-me-me" person who never had time for her kids. He grew up desperate for her love and attention. Now I could sense that same desperation in him for me. Unfortunately, at the time, I confused desperation for love. He went on and on about how sorry he was and promised never to do anything like that again. "Let's plan the big Christmas Eve dinner you want to host," he offered. And we did.

I first saw porn on Rob's computer when I was eight months pregnant. At first glance, I didn't think much of it. We sometimes enjoyed watching a softcore movie together. But WOW, what I saw as I clicked through the open tabs made me cringe. S&M, bondage, degradation and humiliation on a level I had sort of heard about but had never seen or imagined. I didn't know how to bring up the topic with him, or even if I should try to discuss it. He did not want me touching his computer, telling me he had confidential files on it that he often worked on at home. It was not my intention to look at his computer. I was looking for something on the desk while he was in the bathroom and I accidentally bumped it. The computer screen blazed to life. I decided not to say anything to avoid aggravating him, but it continued to niggle at me like a slightly twisted sock in a shoe.

Emmalyn was born two days before Valentine's Day. Rob and I were both thrilled ... at first. The interrupted sleep and my single-minded focus on the baby quickly took its toll on Rob. I had taken to calling Emmalyn "my precious valentine." Two weeks after she was born, Rob said in a voice that was both snarky and sad, "I thought I was your 'precious valentine.' I guess those days are over – forever. The day that is supposed to be about your husband will always be about her."

I decided to plan a belated Valentine's Day celebration for Rob. Mom was thrilled when I asked her to take Emmalyn for four hours. Ever since the cookie incident, I saw a lot less of Mom because I was always anxious about a possible clash between her and Rob. I packed the diaper bag complete with a bottle of breast milk, made an easy meal, got out some candles, and put on a loose-fitting but low-cut tee-shirt since my post-pregnancy body wasn't ready for sexy lingerie.

Rob reacted just the way I hoped. He was very appreciative of my efforts and we went straight to the bedroom. I reminded him that it was too soon for me to have sex, but I was looking forward to having him in my mouth, knowing that he relishes a good blow job. Rob always liked my breasts, especially my nursing-enhanced breasts. The attention he was giving them caused my milk to flow, and surprisingly, he lapped it up. I asked him to stop knowing Emmalyn would be hungry when she got home. That frustrated him but I immediately took him in my mouth. He stopped me after a minute saying if he couldn't have my tits or my pussy, he wanted my ass. This was a long-standing source of tension between us. I had reluctantly agreed to anal sex a few times when I'd had plenty to drink, but I did not enjoy it. "I am still pretty sore down there and I have had problems with hemorrhoids," I said, thinking that would put him off. He replied, "I'll use lots of lubricant and I'll be fast," then flipped me over and went for it. He was so sweet afterward that I did not regret the episode, although I did wish it had felt more loving and mutual. Rob gushed over Emmalyn when Mom brought her home, and he thanked Mom profusely for babysitting. I realized that making sure Rob was satisfied with our sex life was crucial to our happiness.

I wanted a dog for Emmalyn. My best friend growing up was a kind, friendly, outgoing girl named Madeline Snowden. In my mind, Madeline's family was the perfect family. It was as though they had stepped out of a TV show in the tradition of *The Brady Bunch, Eight Is Enough*, and *7th Heaven*. The Snowdens had a beautiful golden retriever. That pooch was full of life and love, just like the entire brood. I equated happy families with dog-owning families. Rob wasn't thrilled about the idea. He didn't want the expense, the dog hair, or the hassle of daily walks and housebreaking. I promised to be 100% responsible for the puppy. Rob relented.

We found an adorable free mixed-breed pup one Saturday from a woman giving them away outside the pet store. She also told us about a discount vet. I assured Rob we didn't need anything but food. I would use old bowls at home for food and water. A couple of Emmalyn's toys could become dog toys. An avid *Star Wars* fan, Rob commented that the puppy reminded him of a miniature Chewbacca.

I suggested Chewbacca as a name, Chewie for short. Rob softened and Chewie came home with us.

It was spring and I was outside with Emmalyn and Chewie. A pregnant neighbor a few doors down was outside with her two-year-old son. Natalie was great, even though she was almost ten years older than I was. Her baby, a girl, was due in a few weeks. I was excited to make a new friend, one with young children. My friends and I had drifted apart again. Now that I was married and a mom, I just didn't have much in common with college students. Rob regularly remarked about how immature they were, always out drinking and partying. I felt like he exaggerated their partying behavior, but I understood his point.

The puppy lived up to his name. He chewed everything – Emmalyn's blankets, the bathroom rug, socks, anything left on the floor. The bigger he got, the more damage he caused. Late one afternoon I was frantically polishing one of Rob's nicer shoes that Chewie had dragged from the closet, trying to hide the teeth marks, when Rob got home. "That's it!" he roared. "Get rid of that little shithead!" as he roughly picked up and flung Chewie into the backyard. Chewie yelped in pain. Rob slammed the door. I started outside but Rob was shouting that he was sick of coming in last. "You care more about everyone else than you care about me; even the fucking dog gets more of your attention than I get!"

I was torn. Chewie might be hurt and needed attention. But was Rob right? Is that why he had been so short-tempered lately? I had to admit that the baby and puppy took a lot of time and energy. By now Emmalyn was crying. I needed to attend to her while getting Rob's dinner on the table. I would check on Chewie later.

The next thing we knew the cops were knocking at the door. Apparently, a neighbor heard shouting, doors slamming, the dog yelping, the baby crying, and called the police.

I was mortified. Rob, however, was calm as could be while explaining to the officer that he had had been playfully rough-housing with Chewie when he accidentally tripped as he was going out the back door and dropped the puppy. By that time, I was holding Chewie who seemed very content curled up in my arms. I assured the officer that Rob's version of what happened was correct and all was well. The officer wished us a good evening, while simultaneously responding to something on his radio as he left.

Rob was obsessed with figuring out which nosy neighbor had called 911. He was incensed. "Who the hell do they think they are?"

Chewie whimpered in the night, not because he was hungry, lonely, or needed to pee. He was in pain. "I think he needs to go to the vet," I said around midnight. Rob replied flatly, "There's no money for a vet." I pressed the issue. The intensity in Rob's voice increased, "That dog is more trouble than he's worth, just like I said from the beginning. He ruined a pair of expensive shoes, peed on the carpet. For God's sake, the cops were here because of him." I wanted to say that the shoes were fine – I had buffed out the minor chew marks. I wanted to say that the cops were here because of him, not Chewie. Instead, I kept quiet. "You said you would be responsible for the dog and you've done a piss poor job," Rob continued. I could see the writing on the wall. Chewie would be better off with another family and then I would have more time to devote to my family. I took him to the shelter the next day, lying that I had found the puppy and he seemed to be hurt. I texted Rob to let him know the dog was gone.

Late that afternoon my mom appeared at the door. "Surprise," she said, "Rob is taking you to dinner and he called me to babysit. He told me you took Chewie to the shelter and are feeling down. He wanted to do something to cheer you up. Get dressed. He'll be here in 30 minutes. You're right, Suzanne, Rob seems to be a good guy. I believe he is really trying." I was happy. Rob and Mom seemed to be on a better relationship footing, and he was being very sensitive to my feelings.

The next day, Natalie and I were taking our routine morning walk. We had missed the day before because I was busy taking Chewie to the shelter. When she asked me about the dog, I told her the story Rob had told the police. She said that wasn't quite the version she'd heard from our next-door neighbor, Marta Olsen. The Olsens were a retired couple in their early seventies. Apparently, Mrs. Olsen had been outside and heard Rob yelling and Chewie squealing. She called the police. She also spoke to Natalie because she knew we were friends. Mr. Olsen urged his wife not to get involved, but Marta was an animal lover and was not going to ignore Rob's outburst. She had already been concerned about the yelling she overheard from time to time.

I reassured Natalie all was well. Yes, Rob could be a yeller, but Marta had misunderstood what had happened. I went on to regale Natalie with the details from Rob's and my lovely evening, from him arranging for Mom to babysit to the delicious meal we ate. Natalie persisted, "But you love that dog." "I do, but what was I thinking trying to housebreak a puppy and deal with a newborn?" I replied. "Now just isn't the right time."

Everything seemed to settle down at home. Rob no longer returned after work in "inspector mode," assessing potential Chewie damage. He still had his standards for what the house should look like and how I should spend my time, but I had learned from watching my mom and dad about how to meet a husband's expectations.

Fourth of July was coming up and Natalie and Jake decided to organize a block party, even though she had just had her baby. They went all out, even ordering a bounce house for the kids. I was looking forward to it. Although I spent time with Natalie during the day, Rob and I didn't socialize much. He got all the socializing he could handle at work.

I wanted a new sundress for the party. I hadn't had any new clothes since before I got pregnant. My maternity clothes had mostly come from thrift stores. Rob hated that I shopped in thrift stores, but he also gave me a very tight clothing budget. We agreed there was no point in spending a lot of money on clothes I'd wear for only a few months. Then, when I would show him one of my $2 Goodwill finds, he would *jokingly* call me a "dumpster diving diva," but in such a disparaging tone, I knew it was not a joke. I ignored him, but it was confusing.

I bought a new dress. If I do say so myself, it looked good on me. My body had rebounded. I modeled the dress for Rob and he was delighted. "I have the hottest wife on the block," he said as he hugged me. Then he saw the price tag. "Fifty dollars!?!" he roared. I replied, "Yes, but it was originally $100. I got it on sale for 50% off. Besides, I planned to leave the tag on and return it after the party." That last sentence spilled out. It had not been my plan to return the dress, but I wanted to calm him down. "I know you're tired of seeing me in 'thrift store trash'," I continued. He did calm down.

We had fun at the party. People were playing horseshoes and cornhole. Kids were running around. There were mountains of hamburgers, hot dogs, potato salad, watermelon, and desserts. Rob and Jake seemed to get along great. Rob drank a lot of beer. He didn't drink regularly, but when he did drink, he drank a lot. I was sitting in Natalie's back yard under an elm tree with some other women when Rob and Jake wandered back from whatever game they had been playing. Emmalyn was hungry, and I was nursing her discreetly, covering myself with her blanket. She flailed a bit and briefly pulled the blanket away. I quickly rearranged it.

It was late when the last of the neighbors went home. I told Natalie I would be back in the morning to help her finish cleaning up. Rob cheerfully wished everyone good night, but as soon as we walked in the door, he started in. "It isn't enough that your tits were nearly hanging out of that dress all day?! You had to show them off to everyone?!" Rob accused.

"I was nursing your daughter, not showing off," I retorted.

"That's a convenient excuse," he snarled. "I saw the way you kept smiling at Jake. Isn't it a coincidence that the blanket fell away just as he walked up? We aren't having sex as often as we used to. I thought you were too tired because of Emmalyn, but you're fucking him, aren't you?"

I was incredulous. "You think I'm screwing my best friend's husband!?" Then Rob lost it. He was screaming once again about how I thought of everyone else before I thought of him. He smashed a picture of me with my mom as he screamed at me, "You fucking bitch." The malice and deliberation of that act scared me. As I turned to run into the bedroom, Rob grabbed the back of my dress and rammed me against the wall, and then he went into the bedroom himself and locked the door.

I went into Emmalyn's room where, thankfully, she seemed to be peacefully sleeping. Remembering the many nights I listened to my parents fight, I made a decision to nip this in the bud. I turned up the white noise machine and called 911. The dispatcher wanted me to keep talking after I gave her my initial report. I told her I was worried Rob would hear me. She said I could give one-word replies to her questions and instructions. Were there weapons in the house? Yes? A handgun? Yes. More than one? No. A hunting rifle? No. Is anyone else in the house? My baby. A boy? No. Is she okay? Yes. Is she with you? Yes. Can you unlock the front door? Yes. It was both terrifying and comforting to have her on the other end of the phone.

When the police arrived twelve minutes later, I was already second guessing myself. Rob seemed to have calmed down or passed out. Had I made an impulsive decision and called when I didn't need to? Too late – they were here. I described what happened. The officers saw the shattered picture frame. One noticed that my dress was torn. "That must've happened when he grabbed me and pushed me into the wall," I said. So much for returning the dress to the store – oh, God, was I really worried about that right now? I was.

Officer Jefferies knocked on the bedroom door. There was fumbling, but soon enough Rob emerged. It was his turn to be incredulous. "We had an argument and I accidently knocked over the picture; then I went to bed. That's all," he told the officers. When they told me that Rob was being arrested for harassment and criminal mischief, I was shocked. I just wanted them to tell Rob his behavior had to stop. I wanted him to have a wake-up call, not be arrested. "Sorry," said Officer Jefferies. "There is probable cause to believe that he committed a domestic violence crime. It's out of our hands. We have no choice but to arrest him."

I was asked to write a Victim Impact Statement and was given a bunch of paperwork. Rob would spend the remainder of the weekend in jail and would see a judge Monday morning. Thirty-six hours from now. What should I do? Should I stay or leave? Rob would never forgive me. My world was suddenly upside-down. I had not thought this through. I sifted through the paperwork the cops had left. They had said something about a protection order. What did that mean? If he could not come home, where would he go? We couldn't afford for him to live someplace else.

In the stack of papers, I found a number for the local domestic violence crisis line. I called to ask questions about the protection order and was asked to give a brief overview of the incident. Instead of just telling the highlights, I found myself spilling lots of specifics about the evening and the entire relationship. Hearing the details aloud, almost as though it had happened to someone else, I had a renewed sense that calling the police was the right decision. Rob had to understand that he could not behave that way. But, as the woman on the phone talked about resources and options – she was full of information – I felt more overwhelmed than ever. The mandatory protection order I just received was not the same as a civil protection order. A civil protection order would give me an additional layer of protection. Did I need more protection? I could come to their office and an advocate would help me with the paperwork and accompany me to court. Whoa, I have to go to court? They could also create a personal safety plan. If I wanted/needed to leave my house, they could screen me for safe shelter. Leave my house? If I wanted counseling, she would pass my contact information to the counseling coordinator. Holy crap – what had I done? This was indeed Pandora's box, and I had opened it.

Just then the doorbell rang. It was Natalie. "We saw the police car," she said. I broke down sobbing and told her the whole story. "I knew Rob could be a controlling jerk, and I really started to wonder about him after Marta told me about Chewie, but I had no idea he ever touched you."

"He doesn't ... he hasn't ... until tonight. And it wasn't even the push into the wall that really scared me. It was the way he looked at me when he smashed the picture. I saw pure contempt." Once again, the feeling that calling the police was the right thing had been (momentarily) revived.

Natalie offered to call my mom, but I told her no. I needed to figure out what I wanted to do. I already knew what Mom would say – *Leave Now.* What did I want? Surly this would be a wake-up call for Rob. Or would he go straight to a divorce attorney? Should I get an attorney? Should I go to Mom's and let him live in the house? Hadn't the woman from the crisis line said something about not going someplace he would expect me to go? Yes, she asked me if I had a friend or relative whose address he didn't know. That seemed like an overreaction. He wouldn't come after me or my mom, would he? My head was spinning. Natalie invited Emmalyn and me to spend the night at their house. I thanked her and sent her home. "We will be okay here while I figure out what to do," I reassured her.

I was finally dozing off when Emmalyn awoke. I was in the habit of scrolling through my phone in the morning while I nursed her. Surprisingly, there were several text messages from Rob's brother asking me to call him. I had never met Brian in person, but Rob had introduced us via Facetime, and we had spoken a few times when Rob was talking to Brian and put him on speaker. Ugh, what did he want? The angst I was feeling when I woke up was rising to panic. Best just to call and get it over with.

"Hi, Brian. It's Suzanne," I said.

"Are you and Emmalyn okay?" he asked.

I was relieved to hear concern in his voice. "We're fine," I replied.

"Rob is stressed out. He doesn't remember everything that happened, but he wants me to tell you how sorry he is," he said. Again, I felt relief wash over me. Brian continued, "Suzanne, if this gets back to Rob's boss, he could lose his job. Where would that leave you and the baby?"

31

The certainty I felt last night when talking to the advocate and Natalie began melting into confusion. My doubt intensified as he went on, "Lawyers are expensive. If this goes to trial, it could easily cost $10,000–$20,000."

Memories of my mom's justifications for staying with my dad flooded back to me. I started crying. "I didn't want the police to arrest him; I just wanted them to calm him down… to let him know he'd crossed a line. Oh no, what have I done?"

"Look," Brian said, "I think this can be salvaged. I had a buddy who went through something similar. His girlfriend told the prosecutor she had blown things out of proportion and that she would not testify against him. They dropped the whole thing. All Rob wants is to come home and make this up to you."

A path forward opened. It seems this episode had the desired effect. It was indeed a wake-up call for Rob. "I have a paper here that says I can go to his advisement on Monday. I'll tell them I want this to end," I said. "That's the smart thing for everyone," Brian agreed.

I told Natalie about my conversation with Brian. She urged me to think about all my options a little longer, but it was clear that my mind was made up. She agreed to watch Emmalyn on Monday so I would not have to call my mom. Natalie told me that Jake was done with Rob. I felt myself start to panic. If people treated Rob differently, that would be bad. He would blame me. Plus, that might drive a wedge between Natalie and myself, and she was the only friend I had. "I really hope Jake will give him another chance. A lot of it was my fault. I know how stressed Rob is about money, and I spent too much on the dress. And I need to be discrete when I feed the baby." Natalie rolled her eyes.

"You were being very discrete and you are the most frugal person I know. You never buy yourself anything and the things you buy for Emmalyn come from Goodwill." I let the conversation drop.

Court turned out not to be quite as easy as I hoped. I told the public defender (who seemed to be representing everyone) that I wanted this to end and for Rob to come home. He told me that Rob could likely be released on a Personal Recognizance Bond, but for that to happen he must sign a Protection (aka Restraining) Order with a No Contact Provision, meaning he could not come home or even talk to me. He also told me I could let the judge, prosecutor, and/or victim advocate know my wishes, but that would not really matter until the next court date in a week. A week? What are we supposed to do for living arrangements in the meantime?

A woman behind me who seemed to read my mind said, "No one will come to your house to check to see if you're both there." I looked at the attorney who just shrugged.

So, Rob came home and I stayed there too. Even though the judge made it clear that Rob was the one who could get in trouble for violating the protection order, I was anxious. I offered to go to Mom's, but Rob wanted me with him so he could "show me his heart." He was wonderful, apologetic, and kind. I apologized too for overreacting and calling the police. He bought a new frame to replace the one he broke. He also made a couple of *joking* comments about how I must "love having his future in my hands."

We talked about whether I should accompany Rob to court. He had heard while in county jail that if the "so called" victim did not show up, the charges were automatically dropped. No victim, no crime. I wanted to show my support by going with him and making a public declaration. Rob really appreciated my intentions, so he decided I should go. He thought it would make a stronger impression than me simply staying away.

The courtroom and hallway were filled with people. I told everyone (the prosecutor, victim advocate, and public defender) I had made a mountain out of a molehill and wanted the whole thing dropped.

The prosecutor, Ms. Willard, scared me to death when she looked me in the eye and said coldly, "So, you lied to the police? We could charge you with False Reporting."

My heart nearly stopped. I could get arrested? This had gone terribly wrong. I should have stayed away. "I didn't lie," I protested, "I overreacted. It was not a big deal – it was just an argument like couples have all the time."

"Of course," she replied sardonically.

Long story short, the case was dismissed, and I was not arrested. When I told Rob about Ms. Willard's threat, his response was not the compassionate, supportive reaction I anticipated, but rather a quippy, "Huh, that restores a little of my faith in the justice system."

Did he really say that? Did he think I deserved to get in trouble? "Do you think me being arrested would serve justice?" I asked.

Rob back-peddled, "That's not what I meant. It's just … we both made mistakes on Saturday. Yes, I admit my mistake was bigger, but it takes two people to fight. I didn't deserve to be arrested for a trivial argument. Being in jail sucked. All I'm saying is that if you got arrested, you would know what I went through. I'm not saying that's what I want, but on some level it seems fair."

I could feel it – the beginning of Rob's shift away from loving, supportive husband to put-upon, misunderstood martyr. Why did I fall for his Prince Charming act every single time? When he came home from jail, I genuinely believed things would be different – that he had learned his lesson. I started to slip into my old pattern of placating him. I was about to say how terrible it was that he went to jail and how sorry I was for calling the police, but I had already said that a million times over the past week. So, I sat there not saying anything because I simply didn't know what else to say. To my surprise, the less I said, the more he swung into Prince Charming mode. I softened throughout the day and things returned to normal.

A few days later, Rob suggested I stop spending so much time with Natalie. Although, he said he was grateful it was she and not my mom who babysat Emmalyn while we were at court, he still went on about what a bad influence she was. It was Natalie who encouraged me to buy that expensive dress. Natalie was always whipping out her boobs to feed her baby regardless of who was around. Natalie, Natalie, Natalie. His resentment against her seemed bigger than the grievances he cited. Then it dawned on me – he was jealous of the bond she and I shared. I was glad I had not told him that Natalie wanted me to leave him and move in with Mom, or that she (based on something Mrs.

Olsen said) had suggested he could be reported for animal cruelty. I knew he was embarrassed – I was too – so I promised not to talk to Natalie about our marriage. "Anytime I spend with Natalie will be solely focused on the kids," I assured him.

I pulled away from Natalie. We still walked and chatted together with the kids every morning, but true to my word, I did not talk about Rob and she did not press. I used the same strategy with Mom. Swinging between defending him and complaining about him made me feel like a whiny, indecisive child. It was a relief to shut up. I think it was a relief for them too. They wanted to be supportive, but it was difficult because I vacillated so widely. Besides, regardless of what they said, I knew how they felt about Rob.

Fall was approaching. Maybe an online class? I decided to approach the topic with Rob. He had been in a generally good mood lately. Unfortunately, I waited too long. He came home that evening in a foul mood, complaining that a guy at work was trying to undermine him. Apparently, Joshua embarrassed Rob in a staff meeting pointing out an error in one of Rob's reports.

Rob poured himself a vodka neat. This was never a good sign. Rob had an obsessive almost paranoid side that emerged when he felt criticized. That particular mood combined with alcohol meant trouble. While he continued to drink, I tried everything I could think of to distract and soothe him – dinner, raving about his many wonderful qualities, affirming that Joshua was an idiot, flirty kisses, and sexual innuendo. Then he saw the list I had made of possible online classes. That sent him over the edge. "Are you trying to put us in the poor house?" he raged. "Or are you just creating a reason to get out of the house to meet your boyfriend?"

"Boyfriend?" I asked incredulously, "What are you talking about?"

He replied, "You were all over me just now. That doesn't happen often anymore. You must be fantasizing about someone."

I insisted that I was simply trying to show him how much I love him. "Prove it," he said as he pulled me into the bedroom. Suffice it to say that he was not as careful as he usually was about anal sex.

I was in pain and bleeding, so I decided to go to the emergency room. Rob was passed out. I called Natalie and asked if I could drop off Emmalyn, telling her that my mom was ill. I didn't want anyone to know where I was really going.

I had a rectal laceration. The injury itself was not serious but I felt unnerved. A Forensic Nurse Examiner and a Victim Advocate both came to talk to me. They were genuinely nice, gently prodding me with questions. I told them what happened – Rob was stressed about work, sex always soothes him, he had had a little too much to drink so he wasn't as careful as usual. While this was the truth, I was fairly sure neither of them believed it was the whole story. The nurse explained that if not performed appropriately, anal sex could lead to injuries that carried a multitude of possible horrible complications.

"A loving partner would not put you at risk," said the nurse.

"Oh, he didn't mean to hurt me," I protested.

"What did he mean to communicate to you?" asked the advocate. That question brought me up short. It stuck with me. What was Rob telling me?

They also asked if I felt safe going home. Did I? Would Rob be sorry or angry about the cost of an ER visit? I decided that if I was not sure, it was probably better not to go home. I picked up Emmalyn, telling Natalie the baby and I were staying with Mom until she felt better.

Mom was beside herself when I reluctantly told her what happened, although I did not go into all the carnal details. "You have to divorce him," she insisted. I kept thinking about the advocate's question – what was Rob trying to communicate? I was not sure what he was trying to tell me, but the message I received was *I can never do or be enough*. And I was tired of trying.

Mom already had the names of a couple of attorneys whom she had researched. I promised that I would make appointments for consultations after I tried to get a few hours of sleep. Surprisingly, I was able to doze. I awoke to Mom's voice on the phone. When I had not replied to Rob's texts and voicemails, he called her. She confirmed that

Emmalyn and I were there. "They couldn't go home after a night that ended in the ER," she said as she hung up. I felt an incongruous mix of anger, fear, sadness, and gratitude for Mom's declaration.

Thus began a new, seemingly endless litany of texts and voice-mails from Rob proclaiming his undying love, his grief, and disappointment in himself. He claimed he had only a foggy recollection of the previous night, but he was deeply and profoundly sorry. If I agreed to simply meet him for coffee, he promised to stop drinking and go to marriage counseling, two things I had requested for months.

Mom did not want me to meet Rob. I felt obliged to hear him out. To ease her mind, I scheduled meetings with both attorneys before I left to see him. Rob surprised me with information that he had already set up marriage counseling for us the next day through the company EAP. They provided six free sessions. I told him I would go to counseling, but I wasn't ready to come back home. He said okay. He seemed genuinely mortified that he had injured me. "You know I would never do anything to hurt you – the vodka caused me to lose control," he said.

Ginny, the counselor, was a pleasant sixty-something woman with short, curly, salt-and-pepper hair. To my surprise, Rob was up front about his alcohol use, sort of. He told her he did not like who he was when he drank, but he did not provide any details saying only that he became angry and yelled. When Ginny asked for my input, I simply agreed. Ginny provided Rob with information about AA and she gave me information about Al-Anon. She urged us both to try a couple of meetings before our next session, when she would begin helping us with communication. I left feeling very hopeful. It was unlike Rob to admit to any flaws, and he had agreed to go to an AA meeting. This was tangible progress.

"Let's go to dinner," Rob suggested as we walked to our cars. "Okay," I agreed. He took me to my favorite old-world Italian restaurant, the one usually reserved for my birthday. He passed on the beer and wine. "Please come home," Rob whispered as he held my hand across the checkered tablecloth. "Things will be different. Haven't I proved that?"

"He's made promises before, just like your father did in the beginning," Mom said when I told her about the successful meeting with the therapist.

"Yes, but he actually went to counseling and agreed to AA," I countered, "Dad never did anything like that."

"I hope for Emmalyn's sake you're right," said Mom in a voice dripping with resignation. "I don't suppose you'll be meeting with either of the attorneys," she continued.

"I think it would be premature," I replied.

So, life returned to normal. Rob was wonderful and nurturing with Emmalyn and me. Here, again, was the man I'd fallen in love with. Natalie and I also continued our routine. She asked about my mom, still under the impression Mom had been sick. I felt bad lying to Natalie, but I was too humiliated to tell her what really happened. Predictably, my internal withdrawal from both Natalie and Mom grew. I felt heartbroken from missing them, but I had my adoring, affectionate husband back.

Frankly, I wasn't sure Al-Anon was for me. It was obviously helpful for many people because both meetings I attended were packed. They were warm and welcoming. The literature was helpful. It was the structure of the meeting I found wanting. I could see how a sponsor could be valuable, though. It made sense to have someone who had been through it help me *work the steps*. Maybe I would reach out to a woman with whom I felt a connection, Mary. She had been married to her husband for over 40 years. There was hope.

"AA is bullshit. Hi, my name is Joe and I'm an alcoholic," Rob said mockingly after dutifully attending his second meeting.

I shared with him how I felt, agreeing that the meeting structure was weird. "But I thought I might ask Mary to be my sponsor. She and her husband have been making it work for 40 years."

"I am NOT getting down in the gutter with any of those pathetic failures. I don't know why you'd want to either." Rob retorted. Then, in a calmer voice, "Besides, I've stopped drinking, which shows I'm not an alcoholic. We'll get some communication tips from Ginny and move on."

Ginny took us through some exercises designed to create and express empathy for each other, which actually seemed really helpful in the office. We were supposed to practice at home, but between Rob's work schedule and Emmalyn, the only time we had was late in the evening when we were both tired. Rob had to cancel our next appointment, and we never rescheduled. So much for counseling.

Things were getting worse for Rob at work. He felt scrutinized and was putting in more and more hours. One night after getting in around 11:00, he went straight into the shower. I got up to use the bathroom, first opening the shower door and greeting him with a kiss. Just then, his phone lit up. I glanced down and was devastated to see the text message from someone named Miranda: "I miss you already."

Rob was unaware there was a message, much less that I had seen it. What to do? Confront him? No, confronting Rob was never a good idea, but I needed more information.

"You're cheating on me?" I asked, dumbfounded. Rob, dripping wet, stepped out of the shower and tried to grab his phone. I walked into the living room scrolling through the text thread.

"Give me my phone," he shouted.

"Asshole," I shouted back.

A screaming match ensued. I was quoting portions of the disgusting messages, while he told me what a lazy, sexually withholding, gold digging, selfish bitch I was.

I called him a pervert and said I had seen his repulsive porn. "Mom and Natalie were right. I should have left you a long time ago." That's when I saw it in his eyes – cold fury. I was terrified. He was coming toward me and I turned to run. He grabbed my arm and pulled me toward him. As I spun around, I instinctively hit him hard in the face with the phone that was still in my hand.

Blood started pouring from his nose. He pushed me down hard and went into the kitchen. "Fucking bitch," he said.

I followed. "I'm so sorry," I cried, "I didn't mean to do that." I put ice in a plastic bag, grabbed a kitchen towel, and tried to tend to his face, but he pushed me away.

The next thing I knew, the doorbell was ringing. The officers explained that there had been a call about a disturbance. Blood saturated Rob's shirt and the towel. His nose was still bleeding. They separated us, asking what happened. I explained about the text, that I had confronted Rob and we argued, culminating in me hitting him with the phone. They arrested me for Third Degree Assault and Harassment, letting me know that if Rob's nose was broken, the charge would be enhanced to Second Degree Assault, a felony.

3

Psychological Commentary

Janet Kerr

Suzanne's story, though fictional, is representative of many aspects of domestic violence situations that I have encountered through my work with victims and offenders. Power and control are at the core of the vast majority of these cases. The "need" to control is the perpetrator's core issue, and it is manifested in multiple ways. Physical violence is one way, but not the only way. However, once there has been an incident involving physical violence, the threat of that happening again is often terrifying for the victim and serves to strongly influence her choices.

Tactics to develop and assert power and control are many and varied. However, there are several that seem to be used commonly, as seen in Suzanne's relationship with Rob, her husband. Among these are financial control (Suzanne must account for every penny she spends and is constantly berated for spending too much), isolation (Rob tries hard to drive a wedge between Suzanne, her mother, and her friend Natalie), and emotional and verbal abuse (Rob belittles Suzanne, baselessly accusing her of flirtations and affairs). He refuses to allow her to continue her education – citing financial constraints. This serves to limit her ability to develop her own agency and reinforces her isolation.

We see early on that Rob is trying to isolate Suzanne. Observe the incident of the concert tickets. Rob seeks to prevent Suzanne from meeting with her friends by showing her concert tickets he says he has bought for her. She believes it to be a nice gesture, and she cancels with her friends to accommodate Rob, only to find that he had lied about when he had bought the tickets. We can see that this bothers her, but she "lets it go." Letting things go a bit at a time leads to habits of appeasement. Later, when Suzanne discovers very hard-core pornography on Rob's computer, she chooses not to confront him. She has learned to avoid confrontations by looking the other way.

Perpetrators can be experts at manipulation – they can keep their targets off balance by alternating between moments of flattery and generosity and moments of cruelty and irrational behavior. The victim therefore is never sure what to expect. "Walking on eggshells" is an expression victims commonly use to describe this feeling of vulnerability and unpredictability. We can observe these behaviors in the first incident when Rob explodes at Suzanne – as she forgets her glasses as they are going to the movies. He calls her manipulative, "just like Amanda," (his former girlfriend). This takes her by surprise – she doesn't understand where it is coming from. However, he apologizes by treating her nicely at the movies, and she decides that his outburst was a strange aberration.

A perpetrator frequently perceives rivals for the affection and attention of the victim who will detract from his primacy. The victim is therefore continually called upon to reinforce her devotion to him. His need for attention seems to be bottomless, and a victim often tries repeatedly to reassure him that he "comes first." Rob even manipulates Suzanne's love for their baby, Emmalyn. Recall the Valentine's Day incident where Rob accuses Suzanne of deposing him as her "valentine," in favor of their daughter. The result is that Suzanne will lead a life of trying to "apologize" for her "shortcomings," and she will accede to sexual activities that she does not enjoy in order to "prove her love" for Rob. Notice that sex between them has always been described as edgy. Suzanne has been pushed out of her comfort zone to engage in sex that is not a connection or a merging, but that has elements of dominance, roughness, and again, control.

Suzanne has learned behavioral responses to abuse through her personal family history. Not all victims have come from families where abuse was present, but this is more common than not in domestic violence cases. We see in Suzanne's story that her family dynamic – her dad's abuse of her mother and her mom's response – conditioned her to adopt placating behavior. She was admonished to be careful when "Dad was in a mood." She was never to leave toothpaste in the sink. The term we use in describing the way that this contributes to an escalating DV scenario is "the enforcement of trivial demands." The more one agrees or gives in to seemingly trivial demands, the easier it is for a perpetrator to assume more control. Accommodating becomes the norm. Her mother, though suspicious of Rob and worried for her daughter, declares on one occasion that Rob really seems to be "trying." Does she really believe that, or is she just pretending – continuing patterns that were prevalent in her own marriage?

If Suzanne's story is to be used as a cautionary tale, we can see "red flags" in almost every paragraph. How can one tell if a relationship is heading into dangerous territory in terms of power and control issues? First, such relationships often develop at an unnaturally quick pace. Suzanne's pregnancy almost traps her into a marriage for which she knows she is not ready. Did Rob intend this to happen? We can't know for sure. But this aligns with a common theme – perpetrators often, if not almost always, have a deep fear of abandonment. They seek someone to fill this deep void. They therefore hasten to cement a relationship quickly and will resist efforts to slow things down or create space for their chosen partner. These relationships often exhibit a "honeymoon phase," when everything seems to go smoothly and the perpetrator exhibits loving behavior that often convinces the victim that he is a thoughtful and accommodating suitor.

Note also, in Suzanne's story, Rob's perception of his past failed relationship with Amanda. He takes no responsibility whatsoever for his part in its failure, branding it "all her (Amanda's) fault." In the first instance when Rob exhibits rage, the glasses incident, he brands her with the worst criticism he can think of – "You are just like Amanda." Suzanne then seeks to prove that she is NOT like Amanda, and tries to adopt the behaviors that Rob prefers. After especially inflammatory episodes, when he seeks to win her back, his apologies can sound sincere. Perhaps the offender really does not like his own behavior. But as soon as the victim is brought back "under control," self-righteousness is reasserted.

Suzanne clings to her desire for a wonderful family, with strong traditions, especially involving holidays. She hopes for a nuclear intact family, and believes that is a realistic expectation if she can only "manage" the difficult times, complying with his sexual demands and being careful about finances and other things that seem to be important to him. In everything, she sublimates her own dreams and desires, seeking only to appease or please him.

Rob understands that Suzanne's relationship with her mother is her primary source of support, and therefore he tries to drive a wedge between them. It is interesting that the first physical incident between them involves Christmas and Suzanne's mom – both so important to Suzanne. Recall that Suzanne and her mother have been having a great time together making Christmas cookies. Rob disparages their efforts, and after the mother departs, he tells Suzanne that her mother has "sassed him," throwing a plate of cookies, shattering it, and demanding that she clean up the mess. Notice also that Suzanne's mother seems unconcerned during the incident – she has been thoroughly conditioned to accept bad behavior. Suzanne is concerned, however. She doesn't want her daughter to grow up in a home full of conflict. She decides to "nip it in the bud" and leave. Some victims try to leave early in a relationship; some leave and return; others stay for much longer, enduring more and more. Suzanne is an example of a hybrid reaction; she leaves, but she goes to a motel so their dispute will remain private. She leaves open the possibility of reconciliation, and in fact, Rob seems frantic and full of regret when they communicate. Suzanne confuses his desperation for her with love.

It is also not uncommon for a perpetrator to view a child as competition. This can be exacerbated if the child is not biologically related to him. It is also not uncommon to see strong preferences for a particular gender in a child. The birth of a baby and the accompanying demands of parenthood can produce tremendous stress. Jealousy can be a strong complication. Suzanne wants to prove to Rob her "prioritization" of his feelings after his remarks about her preference for the baby over him during the Valentine's Day incident. When she asks her mom to babysit and acquiesces to his sexual preferences, he again assumes control and can afford to be kinder toward her.

The situation with Chewie, Suzanne's beloved puppy, is very important. There is a strong correlation between abuse of animals and abuse of children and partners. Once again, it is all about control. Although Rob couches his complaints about the dog in terms of finances, dog hair, and destructive puppy behavior, in reality he sees that the dog diverts attention, and in his view, affection, from him. Hurting the dog sends a powerful message to Suzanne. It demonstrates lack of empathy and a willingness to inflict great physical injury. If Rob can do this to a puppy, she intuitively understands that he can also do it to her if she "misbehaves." Suzanne questions her own behavior, wondering if she in fact was to blame.

This is the first incident in which law enforcement intervenes, after a neighbor witnesses the cruelty to the puppy and calls the police. When they arrive, Rob is a portrait of calmness, and they both assure the police that there is truly no problem. Again we see tactics that Rob employs to assert control – he minimizes, denies, and blames everyone but himself. He insists that Suzanne privilege his feelings over every other consideration, arguing that the dog has even brought the police to their door. Suzanne gives in and returns the puppy to the shelter. She gives up something she really loves, arguing to herself that it was wrong of her to try to raise a new baby and a puppy at the same time, and that she has been unfair to her husband. Rob's explanation of his cruelty to Chewie exemplifies typical offender rationalization: "Nothing happened, but if something did happen, it was minor, and it was not my fault." The repercussions of the intervention of law enforcement, however, are serious, as Rob is furious that neighbors have called the police. His need to isolate Suzanne from her friends and neighbors escalates.

The Fourth of July neighborhood party represents another escalation point in the drama of their relationship. During the party, Rob, who had been drinking to excess, accuses Suzanne of deliberately exposing her breasts as she nurses her baby. These accusations of flirtatious behavior take Suzanne by surprise. She is wearing a new dress that she has just bought, intending to return it after the event. When Rob slams her into the wall and her dress tears, she is so conditioned to worry about finances, that her first thought is, "How can I return this dress now?" She calls the police, seeking only to "scare Rob so he will change his behavior." But this time, Rob is arrested.

As the story proceeds, we see Suzanne's continued reluctance to "hurt" Rob and her inability to navigate the system that is in place to address DV situations. She finds the court appearance and the information she receives from a helpline overwhelming. Rob enlists the aid of his brother to communicate with and plead his case to Suzanne. Brian warns her that if she does not drop the charges, Rob's job is at risk. The family financial situation is precarious, and Suzanne feels she cannot jeopardize Rob's source of income. Once again we witness Suzanne's desire to protect their nuclear family.

Suzanne is also reaching a point where she is becoming uncomfortable sharing her problems with her mother and her friends. She feels she is exhausting them with the sad, repetitive story, and it would be better for everyone if she just stopped talking! This is also a very common manifestation we see in DV situations. Support systems often erode under the strain of trying to help a victim who is struggling.

The incident in which Suzanne is injured by forcible anal penetration is particularly telling. Rob has been drinking when he discovers that Suzanne is once again thinking of enrolling in college classes. He becomes enraged, accusing her of seeking to find a way to meet an admirer. Suzanne tries everything to appease him as the situation escalates – and the result is anal laceration and a trip to the emergency room. After this injury, Suzanne takes her daughter and goes to live with her mother, only returning when Rob agrees to counseling. The counseling is, however, short-lived, as is frequently the case.

When Suzanne discovers that Rob has been having an affair, Rob blames Suzanne with demeaning accusations of sexual inadequacy. The situation escalates, and in the final confrontation in her story, she is a "reactive resistive victim," as she inadvertently injures him in an attempt to defend herself.

As we consider Suzanne's story, many will simply ask, "Why doesn't she just leave?" In fact, many find "staying" in circumstances such as those surrounding Suzanne, completely incomprehensible. So this question of why she, and other victims, remain in abusive situations is extremely important for us to contemplate and try to understand.

If we were to ask Suzanne, she would probably say, "I love him; he can be so great! Yes there are bad times, but there are also good times!" In reality, Suzanne still has a deep yearning for a loving husband and a happy family. Because her father was abusive, she has been groomed to make accommodations to her husband. It feels normal to her, as she does not have other models of behavior in a marriage. She rationalizes that Rob has rarely been physical toward her, and those incidents were influenced by alcohol. She dismisses other examples of verbal and emotional abuse as "isolated incidents" that need to be suffered through to get to the good times. She is ready to assume responsibility for his abusive behavior as he denies, rationalizes, minimizes, and blames. His erratic behavior keeps her off balance, and she finds ways to excuse his behavior. She usually ends up in the place where she feels she must just try harder to make it work.

Her love for Rob, however, is tempered by fear. She sees that he is capable of hurting the dog. Victims instinctively know that injuries and homicides occur most frequently in a DV situation when the victim tries to leave. This is, in fact, an accurate perception. There is usually a "tipping point," however, when a victim makes that choice.

This might come, for example, if a victim fears deeply for the wellbeing of her child or children. Perhaps there has been an incident that has been so terrifying that it represents "the last straw." Nevertheless, the risk of leaving may seem as dangerous, or more dangerous, than the risk of staying.

Finally, there are questions of resources. Rob has total control over their finances, and Suzanne has no degree and no skills. She is lucky in that she does have a place to go if she chooses to leave, as her mother will take her in. Not many victims are that lucky. Still, living is expensive and she has nothing of her own and a child to support. How will she manage? It is humiliating to acknowledge that her marriage is a failure. The privacy of their life together will be shattered along with her dream of creating a solid, happy nuclear family. The outsider looking in thinks the choice is simple. It is not.

I will conclude with the thought that blaming the victim in DV situations is all too common. It is nearly impossible for many to understand "why she stays." They ask, "So is it not her own fault that she is a victim?" It seems to be so easy to just walk away. There are safe houses and police and courts and therapists to support her. Sympathy can evaporate for the woman who returns to dangerous relationships or never leaves them in the first place. Suzanne's story should help us understand the dynamics of how an offender exerts power and control, and why it is so dangerous and difficult for a victim to break free.

4

LAW ENFORCEMENT COMMENTARY

Howard Black

It is a little known fact that traffic stops and domestic violence calls are potentially the most lethal scenarios for law enforcement. In 2019, 40% of law enforcement fatalities occurred while police were responding to DV calls for help. The other little known fact has to do with the sheer numbers of DV calls. For example, in the city of Colorado Springs, current population of approximately 472,000, we have between fifteen and twenty thousand DV calls a year. Each one of them could potentially be difficult and dangerous for the officers involved. Each one requires careful handling, backed by extensive training. Not every call comes encoded as DV. It could be a call about a barking dog. So the actual numbers of DV incidents requiring police response is even higher than the statistics might show.

Let me describe to you what is likely to happen in the course of a routine law enforcement response to a call involving potential DV. If you remember, in Suzanne's story, there have already been two police responses – one to a call from neighbors and one when Suzanne called. First, a typical response requires two officers. However, sometimes one officer has to go in alone, if they have no cover and the situation warrants immediate intervention. You will hear something like, "2 Adam 41 copy 2 Adam and 62 cover. Domestic violence call

4956 Academy Boulevard. Male and female fighting, no mention of weapons." That is all the information you have. The two patrol cars acknowledge and move to the scene. While they are moving, there is a call taker that is still with the victim, just as described in Suzanne's story. The call taker will type real-time information into the call screen, and once the officers get closer, they can read the update of what is happening.

Now suppose shots are fired or the guy has broken into the bathroom where the woman is hiding. The officers are trying to arrive as quickly as possible, with red lights and siren. The first car waits for the second car unless it is a "hot domestic" and he feels he/she cannot wait. 2 Adam 61 will inform 2 Adam 41 that he/she is going in.

In a perfect world, both cops will get there at the same time. The dispatcher might tell you, "Hey, we have previous history there. Check computer information." That's all you have, and you are very careful walking up to the house. You are listening and want to gain as much information as you can before you actually knock on the door. You might hear them yelling. You think there are no weapons. There is no physical injury at this point. The officers will then meet at the door. You announce, "Police Department. Can we talk to you?"

Nine times out of ten it is the male that walks to the front door. The officer might say something like, "We heard that there is an issue inside your residence. We would like to come in and just talk with you." Most of the time you can talk your way in. If the individual cooperates, each officer takes responsibility for half of the area. You do a quick scan. There could be guns, knives, sticks, baseball bats, so you have to be aware and careful. You are now trying to develop a relationship. You want to be sure you are safe, but you do not want to come in heavy handed, guns blazing. One of the first things I always ask is, "Hey, how many people are inside the house?" If we have two individuals that are cooperative, I will want to talk to each one separately. Let's say we have appropriate separation. Then the two officers will come together and compare what they have heard. I can tell you that I have almost never heard the offender say, "I want to take responsibility. I did push her down."

Now you have two stories – his and hers. Let's say the female says, "He got angry at me and shoved me into the coffee table and it knocked over a pot." He is saying, "Yeah, man, I was angry. I got in her face, but I never touched her." You will go to the coffee table. Has something been knocked off? Has the table been moved from its original position? You are trying to figure out who is telling the truth and who is lying. You establish whether you have "probable cause" to believe that a crime has occurred.

In the scenario in Suzanne's story, the potential crime would be harassment. Under Colorado revised statutes 1891-11, if you push, shove, slap, hit, or annoy, it falls under "harassment" under that statute. Colorado is a mandatory arrest state. If police have probable cause to believe that a crime has been committed, you are mandated to arrest. However, harassment is one of the crimes that often requires experience on the part of the police. What I see as probable cause might not be what another officer sees. While we respond to fifteen to twenty thousand DV calls every year, we only average about 3500 arrests each year for DV in the city of Colorado Springs.

In the state of Colorado, harassment is a "custodial arrest ... if DV related." That means that the individual who perpetrated the harassment will be taken into custody and booked in the El Paso County Criminal Justice Center. He will have to see a judge. If he is arrested on a Thursday night, he will see a judge on Friday afternoon at one o'clock. If he is arrested late afternoon on a Friday, he will be in jail until Monday at one o'clock when he will see the judge. During DV calls, harassment and third-degree assault are the most typical crimes to be considered. There are times that both parties are arrested, but that is extremely rare. That is called a dual-arrest case. The officers at the scene have firsthand opportunity to observe what has been going on. They are the ones who really need to make determinations about what has happened. It is important to try to identify the "primary/ dominant aggressor." That can be very complicated. Often the male in the household will try to persuade a male police officer to identify with him. He might say, "You know how crazy a woman can be. You know, like your wife … you know …"

In Suzanne's story, we are dealing with low-level crimes, not felonies. However, it does not matter whether it is a low-level harassment crime or attempted murder. Out of everything that cops deal with, domestic violence is one of the most complicated crimes that you respond to. You are always dealing with two different perceptions. You almost never have unbiased witnesses. You are also dealing with all of those abuser dynamics that occur and all the victim dynamics also. Abusers do a wonderful job telling their story, and they usually are not truthful. They often think that they can manipulate the cops with their stories. I remember one case where we responded to a DV call. When we arrived, the woman was at the doorsteps screaming and yelling – really out of control. When we went inside, the guy was lounging on a couch – feet up, beer in one hand, cigarette in the other. He looked at us and said, "See what I have to put up with? She is totally crazy. I'm not doing anything." Well you can't take scenes like this at face value. When we interviewed them separately, we found that he had thrown her in a closet. Every time she tried to get out he would strike her with a stick and force her back in. That had been going on for six hours. She was badly injured and completely terrified.

Sometimes it is hard to get victims to engage with you at all, often out of fear but sometimes out of *love*. If these are repeated cases, when you have perpetrators who have been through the system, they have learned how to deal with the system. They get better at it. And of course, we know that more victims die once they leave their relationship – that is, when the perpetrator ultimately loses control.

Then you have cops who have their own biases. A cop might be an abuser himself. He might have come from a family where the father was an abuser. Cops can be victims. We have had attorney victims and attorney suspects. We have had professional people and unemployed people as both victims and suspects. Imagine all those different dynamics. And then we ask young police officers to go into homes and sort through what is actually happening.

Here is one scenario that might happen. The officers are called to a scene, they go in, and they know something has happened, but neither the suspected victim nor the suspected perpetrator will talk to you. In this state, the officers can say, "Okay, I am going to force a timeout." The officers will call an on-duty judge and request an emergency protection order where you force a court-ordered timeout. Timeouts can be very important. The officer will call the judge and say, "This is what I am seeing here and this is my recommendation." Then the judge can say yes or no. Usually the judge will support the officer's recommendation.

This is an exceptionally useful tool that was used more frequently in the past than it is now. Some on-call judges don't really like being called ten or twenty times a night to give their approval for these protection orders. In former times, a victim had to sign a complaint in order to get an arrest. Many victims did not want to do that. Their reasons were very complicated. We have come a long way since that time. Now victims do not sign complaints at all. The cops are making that decision as to whether or not to move forward based on probable cause.

Cops receive blocks of training on domestic violence that will include role play and discussion of different DV scenarios. Police academies here are approximately six months long. But most of their real training comes out in the field. They will work with three training officers during the field training. This is where they will see what goes on in the real world. And as I said, every time they answer a DV call, they are walking into a potentially lethal situation. It is a huge responsibility fraught with potential danger.

Suzanne's story highlights one common characteristic of abusers. They often target children and animals, especially pets, to gain leverage over their victims. They use cruelty as a way to say to the victim, "If I can do this to your dog, imagine what I can do to you." It can involve really horrendous animal abuse. I remember a case where an abuser used an ice pick and pierced a beloved horse's hoofs. That horse was lamed forever. Abusers will throw a cat against a wall, killing it. They might cut an animal's throat. We have seen a lot of different perpetrators' strategies in abusing animals. That is why it was so important to include the humane society and other animal welfare nonprofits in our circle of agencies that address domestic violence. Animals frequently become targets of abuse by a violent perpetrator.

I have come to understand more fully the importance of children in DV situations. Parents might think that children don't know what is going on, or that they are too young for tension and abuse to register. That is not the case. Children know; children are impacted. I have walked into so many scenes, and after asking if there are children present, have found children hiding under the covers on their beds or with their heads under pillows to avoid hearing arguments and screams. I try to tell my officers how important it is to acknowledge the kids. They suffer tremendously in a home filled with abuse.

Children are also used as a way to "get at" the adult victim. Sometimes they are targets themselves. There is one case that is indelibly etched in my memory. It is not for the faint of heart. This particular couple had three children – ages 15, 13, and 10. The couple had a long history of DV problems. The man was especially violent and abusive when he was drinking, and the kids knew this from experience. On this particular occasion, the mother was not at home. The guy walked into the house carrying beer and started yelling, "Where is your mother?" Because the mom was not present, he started picking on the 13-year-old, a girl. It was getting nastier and nastier, and hearing this, the 15-year-old went out an upstairs window to call the police. Now here is the amazing part. The 13-year-old had the presence of mind to start a recording, so that every word that ensued could later be heard. The guy started hitting her with his baseball cap – one that was lined with a metal rim. Then he told her to go into a closet and get a rifle that was in there. He ordered her to put the rifle in her mouth and pull the trigger. She kept stalling him, saying things like, "But Dad, my arms aren't long enough." Then she told him she didn't want to make a mess in the living room so maybe they should go in the garage. He actually agreed to that; she knew the police had been called and was hoping to delay as long as possible. He kept telling her to pull the trigger, while continuing to hit her. The cops burst into the garage and apprehended him. Everything was on tape. Everything was there for everyone to hear! And when the police checked the rifle, it was loaded.

It is really something when a judge is willing to go out on the streets with the cops to try to get an understanding of what it is really like to go to a DV call. The judge who is contributing to this book did that when he was Chief Deputy District Attorney! He has seen these things firsthand, and he is one of the few who actually spent time on the streets and really understands what the issues are. I remember one DV case in which we were just finishing up. We had just arrested the perpetrator. The judge – then a chief deputy district attorney (DDA) – was there alongside me, and the perpetrator said (referring to the DDA), "Who is this motherfucker?" And the DDA said, "Well, I am the motherfucker who is going to see you in court tomorrow."

"There is one universal truth, applicable to all countries, cultures, and communities: violence against women is never acceptable, never excusable, never tolerable."

— Ban Ki-moon

VICTIM ADVOCATE'S COMMENTARY

Erika Vida

As a Victim Advocate, I constantly encounter domestic violence (DV) situations. The public would be astonished to realize how many calls to law enforcement involve DV. It is like an epidemic. Some cases have the potential to be extremely lethal. All, however, can be very traumatic and damaging to victims and their children. It can be frustrating and exhausting to intervene in DV situations. Let me give you an example.

Once I interviewed a victim who had obvious physical signs of strangulation – clearly visible bruising and finger marks around her neck. When I started to discuss options available to her as a victim of domestic violence, she said, "But I'm not a victim of domestic violence. The last time he strangled me, it was much worse."

Suzanne exhibits many of the characteristics of victims with which I am very familiar. Rob has taken away almost all of her power and autonomy. She questions whether she can exist without him; she is dependent on his financial support. From the beginning of their relationship, he has said, "I'll take care of you," while using all manner of tactics to prevent her from developing ways to take care of herself. Sometimes blackmail is involved. If you recall, Suzanne's previous boyfriend threatened to kill himself if she left him. The names are different, but the pattern repeats itself.

Many victims fear terribly for the wellbeing of their children. Therefore, they take the whole burden of dealing with the perpetrators on themselves, so he will not hurt the kids. They think the children will be protected; but in my experience, children KNOW. They hear arguments, they feel the tension, and they suffer enormously in DV situations. They want to protect their mothers; they want to stop the violence from escalating. But how can they do that? It is an impossible tragedy for them, and one that can have damaging repercussions throughout their lives.

What is a Victim Advocate (VA), and what does my job entail? A VA is part of the law enforcement system. He/she is system-based and is a "first responder." Prior to 1982, the criminal justice system was really focused upon criminals, not victims. Victims were not aware of their rights – indeed their rights were not clearly codified. Therefore, many if not most victims were very reluctant to talk about the crimes committed against them. They would not report – and this was understandable given the lack of protections and assistance for them. At that time there was also reluctance on the part of law enforcement to intervene in "domestic" or "private" disturbances. Gradually, rights of victims have been recognized and acknowledged, and legislation has been enacted to protect and assist those who have been victimized.

In our local police departments, there are Victim Advocacy Units that can provide support and services to those who have been victimized by crimes detailed in the Colorado Victim Rights Act (CVRA). I am on call 24/7 for Teller County, with an area of 559 square miles and a population in excess of 25,000. I have one part-time colleague (soon to be two) and some volunteers to assist me. I will provide immediate assistance to victims, on the scene, regarding safety planning, and will offer information on the CVRA. I will help victims complete applications for the Victim Compensation Fund, assist with referrals to community agencies and resources, and support them during the investigative process. I will try to help them understand the criminal justice system and how it works, and I can help with translation services when necessary and also with protection orders.

Many more crimes are covered by the CVRA than one might suspect. Those include stalking, child abuse, sexual assault, human trafficking, sexual exploitation of children, violation of protection orders, and domestic violence as well as crimes like first-degree burglary, aggravated robbery, and bias-motivated crimes. Victims have the right under the law to be notified when an offender is released from jail. When conditions are met, compensation is available for victims for losses that include reasonable medical and dental expenses, mental health counseling, and property damage, among others.

When there is a call to law enforcement to address a crime against a person, the victim is asked whether he/she would like a VA to be present. If the answer is yes, I will accompany the police, or go to the scene as soon as possible. My primary mission is to ensure the safety of the victim(s). Everything else is secondary. I must first be sure that any victim knows that whatever he or she tells me that relates to the case is NOT confidential. I am obligated to report it to the police. This is different from intervention by representatives from a typical community-based DV organization, who can keep information confidential. They will not give out information from a victim unless granted permission to do so. I have a duty to report what is shared with me, and a victim has the right to know that.

My feeling is that the group of law enforcement officers I work with is very appreciative of what I do and very attuned to the need for victim advocacy. But this has not always been the case. I remember one officer many years ago, in a different jurisdiction, who said to me, "In my 30 years as a police officer intervening in DV situation, I've never met a true victim." There is plenty of room in plenty of communities for better training of police concerning DV. However, there has been substantial improvement.

Sometimes I find that officers want to rush victims into statements. Victims can be deeply traumatized. They may forget details or be unable to speak coherently about what has happened to them. They might need time to regain strength and remember details. Perhaps they have not eaten or slept for several days. Sometimes I ask the officers to give the victim more time before their statements. I am there for the victims, not the officers – but we try hard to work as a team. I will try to address the victim's immediate needs, "Are you comfortable? Are you safe? Are you hungry? How can I help you?" I will want to know if the perpetrator is in custody. I will ask her about the children, if there are any. I will inquire about her support system. In some cases, I might recommend her moving to a different state altogether, in which case I will try to arrange support for her there.

I might take the victim shopping for clothes or food. She might need to go to the hospital, and if so, I might be the one to take her there and stay with her. In our region, if she does go to the hospital, TESSA, the community organization that addresses DV and sexual assault, will be called. I will step out of the room when that representative arrives to talk with the victim, owing to the confidentiality, non-confidentiality issue. TESSA has many resources with which to assist victims, including a Safe House for temporary lodging for victims at risk.

DV does not discriminate. I've seen cases involving the wealthy and the poor, professionals and unemployed, all races, and all different strata of society. I recall one case where I saw a woman's car parked in front of our offices. It was an expensive car, and I knew who the woman was. I immediately thought, "She is here to make a big financial donation." In fact, she was there to seek assistance. Her husband, a highly regarded professional in the community, tracked every mile she drove on her car's odometer, timed her visits to the grocery store, and examined her phone many times daily to control her interactions with friends and relatives. Just like Suzanne, this woman was being subjected to abuse by her husband, who sought to control every aspect of her life.

Perpetrators have many and varied tactics, but they almost never accept responsibility for their actions. It is not unusual for them to say to a victim, "Look what you made me do." In other words, according to the offender, the victim "deserves what she got." Interestingly, victims will tell me that they instinctively know when tension is building in a relationship. They know that tension will eventually erupt in violence. Sometimes the fear of impending violence is so strong that a victim will actually try to provoke it. "I know it is inevitable. I know it is coming. I just want it to be over!" As we see in Suzanne's story, the cycle of abuse becomes normal for the victim. I try to tell them, "It is never okay for someone to hurt you."

It is hard to understand why many victims refuse to report. My view is that she might not be ready to do so. I have witnessed many victims beaten so badly that they can't open their eyes who still will not leave the perpetrator. She also might be legitimately afraid that the offender will retaliate against her. How many times have I heard, "A restraining order is just a piece of paper? I know he will find me and hurt me."

Things have become even more difficult as a result of the pandemic. Alerting law enforcement to DV and child abuse is frequently done by teachers, neighbors, bystanders, and friends. With limited social interactions, abuse cases are tragically underreported, and victims have far less access to support systems. This is particularly acute in rural areas where families can be extremely isolated. So while statistics may indicate that DV and child abuse cases have declined, in fact, social isolation has resulted in less visibility of abuse, less reporting, and therefore fewer law enforcement interventions. DV and child abuse may actually have substantially increased during the pandemic shutdowns.

I never say to a victim, "I know what you are going through." How could I possibly know? Maybe she has four children and does not know how she will put food on the table, since her husband has taken their stimulus check and gambled it away. How will she keep her kids safe? Maybe she knows that if she confronts him she will be beaten. Maybe he has threatened to kill her if she leaves. I can empathize, but I cannot truly know. I will do my best, however, to ensure her safety. I will help as much as I can.

"Each time a woman stands up for herself without knowing it possibly, without claiming it, she stands up for all women."

— Maya Angelou

6

COMMUNITY RESOURCES FOR VICTIMS OF DOMESTIC VIOLENCE

Janet Kerr

There are hundreds of local, state, and national organizations dedicated to fighting domestic violence. In Colorado alone there are over 40 local programs providing direct services to survivors, including specialized resources for children/teens, differently abled people, people of color, the LGBTQ community, people of faith, and later-life abuse survivors.

These resources typically include: a 24-hour crisis line, emergency shelter, legal advocacy (assistance obtaining protection orders and providing court support), specialized children's programming, individual counseling, group peer support, and transitional housing. Unfortunately, shelters are often full, resulting in thousands of women and children being turned away because of lack of beds.

Because of the subtle and insidious nature of DV, many victims and offenders (and people in general) don't recognize the power and control behaviors that undergird the issue, resulting in people not seeking help until there is a dangerous escalation in conduct.

"Children Learn What They Live" – we all recognize the obvious truth of the statement. In order to eradicate domestic violence, we must ensure our children grow up in homes free of violence and full of respect.

DVERT: Law Enforcement Commentary

Howard Black

O ne of the most promising initiatives to arise out of the need to more effectively address domestic violence was the DVERT Program. DVERT stands for Domestic Violence Enhanced Response Team. This nontraditional domestic violence unit was begun in 1996 in Colorado Springs, and it continued gaining respect nationwide and internationally until it was drawn down as a result of the recession of 2008–9, when law enforcement everywhere was impacted by a drastic decline in resources.

What is the most effective way for policing to reduce recidivism? Recidivism involves the tendency for an abuser to relapse into criminal behavior. That has been a central question in this field for a long time. In 1981 and 1982, the Minneapolis Spouse Assault Experiment, conducted by the Police Foundation, assessed the effects of different police responses to incidents involving DV. Of the three major responses used by police – mediation, separation, and arrest– they concluded that arrest was the most effective in preventing recidivism. This led the National Institute of Justice to fund six sites to replicate the Minneapolis experiment. Colorado Springs was one of those sites (1991 and 1992).

The six replications had different conclusions. Some showed that arrest was not a significant deterrent for misdemeanor spouse assault. Another stated that victims reported that arrest had a strong deterrent effect. Yet another showed that arrest could create even more violence. In Colorado Springs, suspects apprehended for misdemeanor spouse abuse were assigned at random to one of four methods: 1) an emergency order of protection for the victim coupled with arrest of the suspect; 2) an emergency order of protection for the victim coupled with immediate crisis counseling for the suspect; 3) an emergency order of protection only; and 4) restoring order at the scene with no emergency order of protection. The prevailing assumption at the time was that recidivism would be reduced by arresting the perpetrator. It was no easy task to conduct this randomized study. Cops in general are inclined to want to make arrests! The conclusions, however, were extremely interesting. The Colorado Springs study determined that it didn't matter which technique was used. Recidivism remained about the same.

This gradually led the Colorado Springs Police Department (CSPD), with input from various agencies and nonprofits concerned with violence against women and children, to develop a more holistic approach. The Domestic Violence Enhanced Response Team, or DVERT, was born. DVERT provided a multidisciplinary approach to DV, utilizing a collaborative approach involving many community partners. The focus of DVERT was on the safety of the victim, and on utilizing the most effective methods to reduce recidivism. It was a multifaceted approach – seeking to empower victims and provide them with knowledge, support and resources, while using "containment" to persuade offenders not to lapse back into dangerous behaviors.

How do you best prevent an abuser from continuing to perpetrate DV on his victim? DVERT demonstrated that containment can be very effective. In other words, by letting an abuser know that he was constantly being monitored, he could not "isolate" his victim effectively. Isolating a victim is one of the primary goals of a perpetrator. The DVERT program sought to prove that an abuser was less likely to fall back into a pattern of abuse if he believed that his activities were being noticed. Alternatively, an important part of the program involved consistent contact between the victim and members of the DVERT team, who helped with everything from preparing restraining orders to finding adequate shelter.

DVERT started small – a collaboration between the DA's office, the CSPD, and TESSA (Trust Education Safety Support Action, the nonprofit in the city that addresses sexual assault and domestic violence). Its offices were not in the CSPD; it was housed in a different building. However, it expanded to meet the needs of the community. It had a staff of 54 at its height, and eventually worked with 36 different agencies and nonprofits – Department of Human Services, the Humane Society, CASA (Court Appointed Special Advocates for Children), metro city police departments, El Paso County Sheriff's Office, Colorado Legal Services, and school district administrations among others. One of the 4th Judicial District Deputy Attorneys was assigned full time to the DVERT program.

A case could be recommended to DVERT via a form submitted by almost anyone – including school counselors, cops, neighbors, agencies, victims, clergy, and others. DVERT would investigate all relevant material regarding that case – police incident reports, arrests, social workers' reports, etc. Its working group would then meet and review the cases and decide which to prioritize. In some cases no arrests had yet been made. DVERT concentrated on the cases with the most potential for lethality. Cases were divided into three levels – Levels One, Two, and Three. Level One included the most lethal situations in which a victim might be in serious danger. Level One cases were limited to 124 at any given time. From its inception in May 1996 to December 1999, DVERT accepted 421 Level One cases and 541 Level Two Cases. If the team decided to take a particular case, DVERT would take over all aspects of the case, including investigation and advocacy services. DVERT covered two jurisdictions with a population of approximately 600,000. At one time its annual budget was in excess of $1.8 million.

Once a case was selected, the staffing unit of DVERT would make recommendations regarding immediate interventions by the various DVERT member agencies. A multidisciplinary team would be dispatched to address a particular case. The teams would have representatives from law enforcement and several agencies, perhaps including a social worker, therapist, or someone from TESSA. This approach was significantly different from typical police responses where law enforcement predominated. It was a "systemic approach," spreading responsibility for the case among multiple agencies – not just the police. Once the case was in DVERT, ongoing intervention tactics would occur – including counseling, advocacy, shelter, support, and legal services. In some cases, cell phones were given to victims to document telephone harassment and violations of restraining orders. This team would meet individually with the victim and the perpetrator. Some perpetrators would agree to meet; some would not. But if they did meet, there would be packets given out on appropriate and inappropriate behavior, resources, and consequences. The team might recommend a "time out." One of DVERT's most important features was the idea that people cared and the situation was being watched. If a perpetrator were to go "over the line," it would be noticed.

In one of DVERT's first cases, a very violent man in El Paso County who had served time for DV related assault, decided to move his wife out to the Eastern plains in a remote area. He had acreage with a house in the middle of it, and thought he could isolate her where no one could touch him. DVERT decided to take the case when a call came in about screams coming from that home. When the team arrived, the perpetrator said arrogantly, "You can't touch me. You can't be out here." The way DVERT was set up, however, there was great cooperation between counties and municipalities, and police definitely could respond to a call and decide if there was "probable cause." The key message of DVERT was, "We are never going to stop watching you. You can't be invisible."

If there is humor to be found in a DV case, perhaps there is some in this one. Another early case in DVERT involved an abuser who served prison time and was released, time served. It is easier to monitor abusers when they are on parole. This guy was not on parole because he had completed his sentence. There was a protection order in place, and a protection detail was put on the victim and kids. He was not allowed to come within 100 yards of his wife or his children. He rented a house that he thought was 125 yards from the school his children attended. When DVERT learned about this, a detective was dispatched to measure exactly how far the house really was. It was NOT far enough away from the school. After he was confronted, he departed the state.

DVERT teams were essentially multidisciplinary "first responders." Colorado Springs became a national demonstration site for this unique program, drawing attention nationwide – even worldwide. Nobody else was doing it quite like Colorado Springs, and those involved with DVERT were frequently called on to do training and share lessons learned.

DVERT proved to be remarkably successful in many respects. This approach was shown to reduce recidivism substantially. Victims reported feeling safer and more empowered. Violence against women was reduced when a woman became part of the DVERT caseload. Violence against children was also reduced when their mothers were actively involved within DVERT. Those children received increased vigilance, and programs and resources to improve their lives were made available. Coordination among agencies was enhanced. However, as you can imagine, DVERT was very resource intensive – requiring tremendous investment of personnel, time, and money. Today it has largely disappeared as a program. Nevertheless, some of its core concepts persist in the Special Domestic Violence Court. This Court hears few cases – perhaps 20–25 per year. It utilizes a multidisciplinary approach – just as DVERT did – to provide a more comprehensive answer to the problem of domestic violence.

*"Trauma creates change you don't choose.
Healing is about creating change you do choose."*

— Michelle Rosenthall

Judge and District Attorney Commentary

Doug Miles

After law enforcement has determined probable cause and made a mandatory arrest at the scene, the case enters the judicial system. If the alleged crime is a misdemeanor, it will fall to me as a county court judge. If it is classified as a felony, it will go to a district court judge. In this case, Suzanne, in all probability will be arrested for a misdemeanor. The consequences of this arrest in terms of the potential leverage that Rob gains over her are significant. In effect, by arresting Suzanne, Rob has more ways in which he can control and manipulate her. He might say, unless you do X, Y, and Z, I will come in and testify against you. If you do what I want, I will not show up for court. The problem is that if she ultimately enters a guilty plea as part of a plea bargain or she is convicted at a trial, she is labeled as a domestic violence offender. So, from then on, if Rob is arrested for domestic violence charges against Suzanne, if she takes the witness stand, the defense is always going to be, "Ma'am, is it not true that you are a convicted domestic violence offender?"

A District Attorney is the legal representative of the state, whose primary function resides in instituting criminal proceedings against violators of state law. The law of the particular jurisdiction determines whether they are appointed or elected to office and their term of office.

The elected District Attorney is in charge of the prosecuting attorneys, also called Deputy DAs (DDAs). The DA and the DDAs have a great deal of discretion in deciding how to prosecute a criminal case. They can take a case to trial, dismiss a case, or plea bargain. In Suzanne's case, an experienced prosecutor might choose to opt for further investigation of the case, or simply dismiss it. On the other hand, he/she might offer a plea bargain (i.e., plead guilty to the original or a lesser criminal offense with specific conditions such as probation, counseling, fines, etc.) He/she needs to be able to prove a case "beyond a reasonable doubt" in order to be successful in a trial. That is a much higher standard than probable cause. You would be surprised to learn how many cases result in a plea bargain as opposed to trial.

When a person is arrested on domestic violence or sex assault charges, there is no immediate bond. The officer arrests him/her, takes them to jail where they are booked, and they remain in jail until they appear before a judge. The next step is called the advisement. Before the advisement, I read what is called the probable-cause affidavit, which is written by the arresting officer and lays out the factual allegations upon which the arrest was made. In each case it is the court's responsibility to determine whether probable cause exists to support the arrest. The perpetrator then comes before me and is advised of all his rights – right to a trial, right to an attorney, right to remain silent, etc. After that, I advise them of the charges that they have been booked on and possible penalties. Then I address the bond.

My approach is to evaluate lethality and risk in setting a bond. This is considered a best practice around the country. Now we are doing a lot of PR bonds, or personal recognizance bonds, where the defendant is released on their own promise to appear. We are trying to keep people out of jail as much as possible due to the pandemic. However, if I determine the case has a high level of lethality and the alleged victim is at risk of further harm, I may not grant a PR bond. When considering the amount and type of bond, I will also hear from the defense attorney and the DA. The defense attorney will usually be the public defender, who is there to represent anyone in jail if they have no other attorney. By this time, both attorneys will have had a chance to review the probable cause affidavit. Once I hear argument from both sides, I set a bond and I also set the next court date.

Anyone who is arrested for domestic violence must also sign and acknowledge a mandatory protection order before they are eligible for bond. This protection order typically prohibits any direct or indirect contact with the victim, an order to vacate the home, to not possess weapons and, in cases where alcohol or drugs are involved, an order not to use substances. The protection order stays in effect until the end of the case or until modified. Quite a few are modified. Victims have a right to be present at advisements. Sometimes they are present and will ask for the no-contact or the stay-away orders to be lifted. My decision will be based on my determination of lethality. Because I am a county court judge, all those arrested on misdemeanor domestic violence charges will come before me. If arrested on felony charges, the case will be assigned to a district court judge.

At the next court appearance following the advisement, the DA and the defense attorney (or the defendant if not represented) will typically begin plea negotiations. The case will stay on my docket for a month or two while they see if something can be worked out, or if the case will be set for a trial. I won't let them drag out those negotiations for too long, however. Delay is a common practice in these cases, in hope that the victim will not continue to participate.

While this process sounds very straightforward, domestic violence cases present myriad nuances. An officer who finds probable cause for a domestic violence charge must, by statute, arrest that person. Typically, the officers do not drill down very deep into the history of the couple, prior charges, or the context surrounding the alleged offense. They are looking at the facts of what happened that day at the scene. What I do is dictated by state law; our statutes do not define domestic violence in a way that necessarily distinguishes between victims who use violence in reaction to abuse and perpetrators who use violence as a pattern of control and domination. So I have to consider all of the dynamics, expressed and implied, to figure out what is really going on. I consider the accused's past criminal history, and I look at the behavior of the people that are in front of me. If I have a female who has been arrested and a male victim who is there and exhibiting serious dominant characteristics, I will consider that, although the analysis is pretty much the same whether the arrested person is male or female, because of the way the statute is written. The statute does not distinguish between perpetrators who use violence to dominate, control, or exercise power over a victim, or a victim who has used illegal violence in response to prior abuse. However, if a victim is reacting because he/she has been a victim, the jury may find that he or she acted in self-defense, and the verdict will be not guilty.

Our state also has the Domestic Violence Offender Management Board, which sets standards for what kinds of plea bargains can be entered into, or what kinds of programs can be approved for an offender. A DA's discretion is somewhat constrained by these state standards. There are statutory restrictions, also, that limit what a DA can do.

Let me tell you about plea bargains. Of all the cases going through the system, 98% of them will result in a disposition short of trial – either the case will be dismissed or it will be resolved by a negotiated plea agreement. These plea agreements may include, for example, a plea to the original charge with an agreement for probation and no jail, a plea to a lesser charge, or a guilty plea with a deferred sentence (conviction is not put on the defendant's record for a specified period of time and if the defendant successfully completes all the conditions of the deferred sentence, then the guilty plea is withdrawn and the case is dismissed). Suzanne would likely be offered a deferred sentence in this case.

What young attorneys quickly learn is that they will need negotiation skills more often than trial skills. A very small percentage of cases end in a trial. The sheer number of cases versus the number of judges and available days on which to try cases put strains on the judicial system. For a person accused of a crime, the advantage of plea bargain is certainty – the consequences of the guilty plea are spelled out in detail and approved by the judge. No surprises! Going to trial is kind of like rolling the dice. Either you will be acquitted or you will be convicted, in which case all the penalties are then up to the judge.

One thing that I think is important to understand is that most of the DAs and public defenders who handle misdemeanor domestic violence cases are inexperienced, young attorneys. They do not necessarily have the experience or training to be able to see some of the complex dynamics that pertain to domestic violence cases. Suzanne, in all probability would be arrested at the scene. This gives Rob great leverage over her in the future. The DA has great discretion. He may decide to dismiss this case, look into it further, plea bargain, or take it to trial. But in any case, he is likely to be very green. He might not understand how complicated DV cases can be. How can we expect these young law enforcement officers and young prosecutors to manage these very nuanced cases? They simply do not have enough experience and, in my experience, training. I, as the judge, have to rely mainly on the facts and arguments as presented to me by the attorneys. I am not an investigator.

A very interesting concept that was advanced to me is termed the imbalance of fear. A victim may lash out at a perpetrator because of years of abuse. The perpetrator might allege that he acted violently because she has spent years demeaning him. The law talks about behavior – that violent behavior is never appropriate regardless of gender. But in domestic violence cases, gender cannot be ignored. Consider this scenario: a man goes to a bar for a drink after work. He leaves the bar and walks down a short alley to get to his car. Three women approach him from the other end of the alley. They are loud, boisterous, and start making comments about the man. What level of fear does he experience? Now switch the genders. Does a woman being approached in an alley by three men who are loud, boisterous, and making comments experience the situation the same as the man did? What is her level of fear? The reality is that men and women experience physical violence differently. Men are usually stronger than women – so, a blow from a man is not experienced the same as a blow from a woman. An act might be the same, but the experience might be different. Could a young DA wrap his head around that kind of subtlety?

There are different philosophies about how DAs should approach cases – ways of looking at things and exercising prosecutorial discretion. One is the evidentiary approach. As a prosecutor, I might look at the evidence and decide what I can prove. Then I will make an offer based on what I can prove. Maybe that will be an offer to a lower charge. Maybe it will be an offer of probation rather than jail. But whatever the offer, it is based on the single question – based upon the evidence, what can I prove? The other approach sees things in a more holistic manner. This approach is based upon the prosecutor's ethical obligation to "do what is in the interest of justice." Thus, acting as a minister of justice, the prosecutor must answer two questions: 1) Can I prosecute the case? 2) Should I prosecute the case? This approach is much more nuanced. Those who take the first approach will say, "The Legislature has defined this conduct as a crime. What is in the interest of justice is that this person be convicted or held accountable for this crime." That is as far as they go! Not beyond that! The second approach requires the prosecutor to consider many other factors. What will the impact on the victim be? What level of accountability is appropriate? What result will prevent further illegal conduct? Justice, proponents of this approach to prosecution will argue, requires more than a mechanical application of the criminal statutes.

I believe that in our culture there is still an underlying belief that if abuse is that bad, the victim should just leave. It goes something like this. "She could leave. She should leave. She did not leave. She put herself at risk by not leaving. On some level, she has taken on some responsibility for being a victim." Officers, prosecutors, and judges are used to taking control. They might not have much tolerance for someone who would not take control of his/her life. A defense attorney told me many years ago, "Well, she didn't leave. She must like it!"

While people are more politically correct now and might think it, they don't say it. This unconscious bias against domestic violence victims is still held by many officers, defense attorneys, prosecutors, and judges. The underlying assumptions about what DV victims can or should do is, in my experience, more often a result of frustration than an assessment of the victim's actual situation. Victims are influenced by many factors: money, culture, children, transportation, and many more – not to mention the emotional impact of love, hope, and fear. The prosecutor's task of debunking the "she could just leave" argument and educating a jury about the complexities of domestic violence dynamics in the brief time they have to address the jury are formidable, indeed.

We haven't even talked about caseloads. We have green cops, defense attorneys, and prosecutors. But we also have enormous caseloads. My average caseload before COVID was 500 open criminal cases at any given time. Right now, in this pandemic, my caseload is over 900 open cases. I set sixty pre-trial conferences in a morning. Those are the conferences where the arrested person comes in and talks to the DA and finds out what the plea bargain offer is and decides whether he/she wants to take it. In County Court right now there is one DA investigator for ten prosecutors, each with caseloads of upwards of 800–900 cases. For serious cases, like homicide, you need and deserve resources. Resources are so important. We are dependent upon the adequate allocation of resources (victim advocates, investigators, etc.) if we are ever going to be able to deal with the complexities of DV.

Suzanne will be arrested for a misdemeanor. Most misdemeanor cases will be dependent on whether the victim decides to testify. A lot of victims do not show up. We know the background to Suzanne's actions; we were able to see the pattern of abuse develop incrementally. We know the context of her actions. But in reality, the responding officer will not know; the DA will not know; and the judge will know least of all. I will not even see the police reports, only the probable-cause affidavit. So how then do we bring that wealth of awareness, or empathy, into the system? That, I believe is the challenge.

I currently preside over a DV Court that is a problem-solving court. We have a limited number of cases, and the focus is on support, accountability, and victim safety. What I have learned is that many of the offenders also have a story. They can be incredibly damaged individuals, many of whom are terrified that they won't be in a relationship. Their fears translate into blame and abuse – and of course that is never condoned, but we can at least try to understand the abuser in order to better contain the abusive conduct and protect the victim. We cannot treat the perpetrator as a two-dimensional control freak. He has his own history. Some of these guys have never been successful at anything. They cannot keep a job. Most of them have social problems. Most of them have substance-abuse problems. They have developed survival behavior based on their own experiences. I guess the point I am trying to make is that each actor has his/her own story. Our DV Court tries to address much more than just an act and a consequence. It really seeks to treat problems much more holistically.

As a four-phase program, I meet with the DV Court participants weekly, then bi-weekly, then every third week, then once a month as they progress through the program. I get to know them as individuals. I celebrate their successes and address their setbacks. They get to know me and the DV Court team. We provide resources to the participants and to their victims as our resources allow. Every DV Court participant has multiple DV offenses and comes into the program having failed to successfully complete standard probation – often several times. It is a rigorous program, and remarkably, over half have successfully graduated.

When we talk about the shortcomings of the judicial system, I would have to say that our system is built around punishment. There is a consequence for your conduct. If you do this act, you will be arrested and punished for that. The limitation is that we tell people what they cannot do. We do not tell them what they should do instead. We don't give them guidance. "Why not do this instead?" So, I'm hoping that people reading this book will wonder whether there is a better way for us to address these terribly difficult issues – a way that is still fair, but that is more understanding of the people who find themselves in the judicial system and more positive and success-oriented in its approach.

"Survivors of abuse show us the strength of their personal spirit every time they smile."

— Jeanne McElvaney

The Rest of the Story: Law Enforcement

Howard Black

A story like Suzanne's unfolds every day, virtually every minute, in every community in the United States. I believe the most important takeaway from an analysis of Suzanne's Story is that domestic or intimate partner violence is extremely complex. Lower-level cases, such as that portrayed in the story, are particularly problematic. We are used to "BIG" stories, with serious violence. These incidents attract attention and resources and investigative power. But Suzanne's story is important too, and potentially damaging to all concerned. How will her story be addressed?

The best case scenario for any DV incident is a "deep dive" into the circumstances and parties involved. The best case scenario is a multidisciplinary team that might be able to contain an abuser and offer clinical help to victim and abuser alike. Abusers need to be held accountable for their behavior, but a team should have the time and resources to evaluate the dynamics that are going on. Some jurisdictions may have sufficient resources to "deep dive," utilizing the multidisciplinary approach. But this is not common. Most harassment/ third degree assault cases will receive less than adequate attention. And that is certainly understandable if you consider that while officers are attending a DV scene, they are usually simultaneously getting calls

81

to respond to another scene urgently. These calls are stacking up and "no one else is available" to assist.

Under Colorado Law, if there is probable cause, the officers are mandated to make an arrest. That may or may not be in the best interest of the family or community. The DA's decisions are also complex. He/she has to consider the standard of reasonable doubt, but also what is the best decision for the community and the individuals involved. However, if an abuser case does not move forward, that can have consequences also. It might empower a perpetrator to commit further abuse if he thinks, "Yeah....go ahead and call the police. Nothing will happen."

Then there is the problem of victims defending themselves. In some cases, as in Suzanne's Story, she will be arrested. Although she may receive a deferred sentence, in effect the abuser has been granted a menu of options to cement his power and control over her. Should the officers have arrested her? Did they have a choice? Should the DA pursue her case or dismiss it?

In addition to demonstrating the incremental and subtle steps that entrap victims into abusive relationships, Suzanne's Story should highlight to every reader the extreme complexity of domestic violence and the deep need for multidisciplinary approaches to these problems. For these are true victims, often with children, who deserve the best efforts of our communities to help them not only to survive, but to thrive again.

Observations from the Trenches

Patricia L. Lostroh

Suzanne's story is a composite of every victim I've worked with in my 26 years of assisting victims and survivors of domestic violence. It took me back to very specific women and very graphic and horrible images of what they experienced. There was nothing in this story that surprised or shocked me. I've seen and heard it over and over again. There are so many common threads than run through every woman's story, even though their individual circumstances may differ. While reading this book, I remembered them, one by one. The story of the abuse of that dog was especially real. I had a client once whose abusive partner called her on the phone after she had left and had to leave her pet behind. He told her to listen while he beat her dog, and she stood as much of hearing it as she could.

I love the lyrics of the song, "Love Her Before You Judge Her," that open the book. It speaks directly to the approach I use with clients at Genesis House, and earlier at Victim Assistance. I offer my help, my trust, my "believing them" as a first step; then we go on from there. I have learned that the first thing that needs to be done is to address urgent and emergency needs. On first contact with any victim of domestic violence and/or sexual assault, my first question is always, "What do you need to get through TODAY?" I give emergency help with food, baby needs, sometimes medicine, money for gas (if they have a car), and then we start over again the next day. It does not work to talk in big terms about major life or behavior changes when someone does not even have the most basic needs met for food and shelter. And I've learned that whatever we can do today will make tomorrow easier.

The parts about the sexual abuse and injuries are very real and happen more often than any of us want to know. I am currently working with a client whose abusive husband has repeatedly, regularly sexually assaulted her over the course of a 30-year "marriage" (not really a marriage at all). In recent years she has become stronger in resisting his demands on her, but his usual pattern was to expect and demand sex when he wanted it, and he would not let her sleep at all until she relented. She told me she would just somehow "go away in her head" while he assaulted her, and hoped it would be over quickly. She began to lock her bedroom door to keep him out, but even that did not deter him, because he would start in when morning came.

Another victim recounted to me the story of her stepfather's abuse of the three little girls, sisters, when her mother was working nights. When it was "bath time," it would mean that each little girl would be subjected to forcible and violent sex in the bathroom. These were very young children. My client, who remained a friend for years after I worked with her, told me how she would have to stand in line, waiting for him to assault each one. She described the splatters of blood on the shower curtain. These things happened in the 60's, and my friend was finally the one to blow the whistle when she was an older teenager. She had back injuries that required corrective surgeries; she had lifelong trauma from all those years of abuse. It was particularly damaging to her that her mother did nothing to stop this abuse of all the children.

I've seen other cases like this, too. I believe that many mothers do not feel they can stop it, because, of course, they are being abused also. Think, though, about that tragedy. The one who is supposed to love you most and protect you from harm – your mother – abandons her child to the abuser. That reality is one that can cause severe mental, emotional, and psychological damage to any child. My friend spent most of her life waiting for her mother to admit she knew about it. But that never happened.

Another client who was abused for many years had scars on her face. Her husband soaked towels in bleach, and when she came home he wrapped them around her head. The chemical burns required medical treatment – and these were the scars that showed. Think about the scars that do not show.

Hundreds of women have recounted their stories to me, and I wish I had a dime for every one of them who said, "But I Love Him." We need to define love – what it can be and what it cannot include. We need to educate men and women, boys and girls. And too many abused women want the impossible. They want me, or you, or us, or them, or someone to "fix this guy" so he will stop the abuse. And we cannot do that. What I focus on and believe has helped many women is to explain that reality and to encourage and teach them to respond differently. I tell them they cannot change how he is, who he is, or what he does, but they can learn to change how they respond. Very small changes can make a big difference. An abuser always expects the victim to do what she has always done – which always has the same result – more abuse. It is risky to change responses, but sometimes it does seem to work!

For the most part, I have not been impressed with the "men who batter" programs that are quite popular. Most men arrive at these programs because they are court ordered to participate. They soon learn the standards of what they need to say to "pass the class." I have personally seen only ONE man who participated and went on to remain in a marriage that became manageable if not good.

I've seen women do what animals often do who are caught in traps. I was raised "down on the farm" where trapping to sell furs was common "back in the day." My dad would tell us that he had a muskrat or beaver in a trap, but it had chewed his own foot off to get away. The animal was gone; it had escaped the trap, but the foot was there for my dad to find and know what happened. I see women caught in that kind of trap who turn to drugs, alcohol, sex trafficking, criminal acts, mental illness, and self-abuse; they try to survive day by day, but with a loss and injury that never goes away.

I separate our clients into three categories: those needing emergency assistance, those requiring maintenance, and those who are well on their way to a healthy, safe life. You cannot look at a DV situation simply in terms of "fixing" the DV. There may be drug and alcohol issues, child-care problems, children's behavioral problems, and difficult health issues. Many of my clients are in desperate financial circumstances. There are not many job opportunities where we do our work. The victims will probably end up in a minimum-wage or below-minimum-wage job, if they can find any work at all. In many cases, they end up attaching themselves to another man, who might not be any better than the partner from whom they have escaped. Generally speaking, it can take from 5 – 7 years for a victim to achieve stability in her life.

Suzanne's Story should help readers identify "red flags." Abuse can develop slowly and subtly; and in my experience, women tend to minimize the warning signs. They often have been conditioned to be "fixers" and nurturers. So they fail to recognize the red flags of power and control. Thoughtful consideration of Suzanne's Story should be very helpful in illuminating these dangers.

Sometimes I have found that people think stories of domestic violence are "made up." In my 26 years of assisting hundreds of victims, I can assure every reader that these stories are true. We have a massive problem. In my work, my vision is to move victims from dark places to stability and wholeness. I will tell you that I have had many more failures than successes. It is extremely difficult and discouraging work. However, I feel that if my staff and I have changed the life of only one woman, we have changed the lives of future generations.

The Rest of the Story: A Survivor Speaks

Anonymous

What will happen to Suzanne? Will she finally find a way to leave her abusive relationship with Rob? If she does leave, will Rob retaliate with increased violence? If she stays, will things improve for her?

I know Suzanne. Even though she is a fictional character, her story constructed to tell us about domestic violence and abuse, I know her. I understand how her self-esteem has been eroded. I understand how desperately she wants the relationship to work. I know her confusion about why their marriage has become so ugly. I know she feels responsible for much of Rob's behavior. I know she finds herself making excuses for inexcusable behavior on his part. She had a dream about a perfect marriage and a perfect family. That dream persists somewhere deep inside her – she just doesn't want to give up on it. She thinks things can change if only she can figure out how to please him. And sometimes he seems to love her so much.

I was brought up in a family where my mother modeled compliant behavior toward my father, who was not physically violent, but who insisted on complete control of our family. We were afraid of him and his anger, and he never demonstrated true affection toward any of us children. Looking back, I believe I tried desperately to win his approval – which was always out of reach. I also hated conflict and tension, and learned ways to avoid it at all times – a personal trait that persists in me even today. I am not adept at managing conflict.

Like Suzanne, I married a man who seemed to adore me. Our courtship was fast, and he seemed like a perfect match for me – intelligent, handsome, and with solid career aspirations. I clearly remember the first time he hit me. I was so incredibly surprised. I had simply disagreed with something he said. It wasn't even an important issue. He let it be known that he would tolerate no disagreement from me at all, over anything.

The physical violence grew more serious over time; but I think the verbal and emotional abuse was even more damaging. I see now that it was all based on power and control. He could not tolerate any relationships I had outside the marriage relationship – even those with family and close friends. He was jealous of any of my accomplishments. And in general, he really disparaged women – saying the most despicable things you could think of about women's abilities and achievements. He sought to isolate me completely. He insisted that I devote myself 100% to him.

From the beginning of our marriage, he controlled every penny in our household. I worked and turned over my paychecks. He worked for a couple of years, after which he stayed home. I didn't even know how to balance a checkbook! He expressed great dislike of my family and objected every time I wanted to visit them. I remember that I started a babysitting cooperative with four friends of mine. He was so negative toward my associating with these ladies that he insisted I quit. And I did. I tried to avoid making him angry because his rages were terrible. I didn't want to expose our children to them, and so I tried every means I could think of to please him and keep him "happy." Of course, that was impossible. We could never predict what would send him "over the edge." It was like walking on eggshells.

As in Suzanne's story, his apologies after physical violence seemed sincere. Along with the terrible times, there were good times. He could be charming. No one in the community would ever have guessed what was going on in our home. For some odd reason, it was important for me to hide his abuse. I did not want people to think badly of him. Perhaps it was embarrassment; but more likely it was the hope that the abuse would end, if only I could behave perfectly and never arouse his anger.

His "episodes" followed a distinct pattern. The children and I could feel tension building for several days. The explosion would happen and the terrible rage would persist for three days, before it would gradually subside, as we tried desperately to calm him down and appease him. He was a master of the argument. He always had "reasons" for why he was so angry. Perhaps I had smiled at someone too much. Perhaps I had dressed in a way that he didn't like. Of course, I had done that on purpose, he maintained, just to offend him.

He was also a master at finding extremely hurtful and damaging things to say to me. He didn't like the way I talked. He didn't like the way I looked. The criticisms could be brutal. I was sick a lot, and now I think the stress of the abuse must have affected my immune system. One time, when I was hospitalized, I remember he brought me a cactus. He said it was what I deserved – not flowers. It shouldn't have hurt my feelings as much as it did, but it crushed me.

He had been in the military, and he told me that he could hurt me in ways no one would ever see. And he did. For a long time, the only person who knew about his physical violence toward me was our family doctor. He told me once that after he retired, my files were the only ones he kept. He thought the violence might escalate even further and wanted photographic evidence. I remember another time when I was in the hospital, my husband came into my room and just harangued me. I don't remember what had made him so angry. After he left, when I was in tears, a nurse came in and asked me if there was anything I wanted to talk about. I said no.

I left many times – sometimes with the children, sometimes without them. One time I took them out of school and we went far away. I didn't have any idea how I could actually leave the relationship. I didn't have any money, and I was very afraid that he would retaliate violently. He threatened to do that, and I believed him. So I always went back – waiting until he had calmed down and assured me that "it would never happen again." I never contacted the police. I didn't know that such a thing as a restraining order existed. I felt trapped and hopeless.

When I look back on those years, I am astonished at my weakness. How could I have subjected my beloved children to the tension in the house? Why couldn't I have protected them more than I did? Why didn't I stand up for myself in the face of such insulting, demeaning, cruel behavior? Current medical thinking says that domestic violence can lead to PTSD. I definitely have lingering effects from the abuse. A year ago, my nightmares were so debilitating that I sought help from a therapist who treated me with EMDR, Eye Movement Desensitization and Reprocessing Therapy. This treatment, in the hands of the very skilled therapist, really helped, and I hope that anyone who has experienced difficult or prolonged abuse will try it.

I left our relationship after I got a job out of state, and for once I had my own money. I continued to send him money for several years – that's how tied to him I still was. By that time the kids were grown, out of the house, and self-sufficient – so I was not as worried for them. At one point I said to myself, "I don't care if he kills me. I can't do this anymore." I sought a divorce, asking for absolutely nothing. It was uncontested.

So I know Suzanne. I became "upset" with her as I read her story. "Don't stay, Suzanne. It will only get worse. You can't please him. You can't change him. Find the courage to leave."

But I don't think she will. I wish she would; I wish she could. She undoubtedly still loves her abuser and to some extent can't help but blame herself for what has gone wrong. She doesn't want to let go of her dreams of the perfect family. She thinks things will get better. But they won't. Maybe the only hope for her happiness is an intervention of some kind – by a therapist, a victim advocate, or a social worker. I see a glimmer of hope there for Suzanne. There are people out there willing to help.

I just hope her story demonstrates in some way the web an abuser spins around his victim – isolation, disempowerment, threats of harm. Why can't she "just leave?" Do we blame her for staying? And that is not fair. Perhaps you can now see how difficult and full of danger leaving would be for her. Perhaps you can see how isolated and powerless she has become. These situations are incredibly difficult and complex. Just as I should not blame myself for staying in my marriage as long as I did, we should not blame Suzanne. We should not blame the victim. It is time not for judgment, but for compassion.

"*To be rendered powerless doesn't destroy your humanity. Your resilience is your humanity. The only people who lose their humanity are those who believe they have the right to render another human being powerless. They are the weak. To yield and not break, that is incredible strength.*"

— Hannah Gadsby

Resources

National Domestic Violence Hotline: 1-800-799-SAFE (7233)

Loveisrespect.org (Dating Abuse Helpline): 1-866-331-9474

National Coalition Against Domestic Violence: www.ncadv.org

CDC, National Center for Injury Prevention and Control, Division of Violence Prevention: www.cdc.gov/violenceprevention

Domesticshelters.org

Stopabusenowcampaign.org.

UN Women: www.unwomen.org

Colorado

TESSA: 24-Hour Safe Line: 719-633-3819

Colorado Department of Human Services, Domestic Violence Program

Colorado Coalition Against Domestic Violence: www.violencefreecolorado.org

SafeHouse Denver: 303-318-9989

Stand Up Colorado: 855-978-2638

Violence Free Colorado: 888-778-7091.
Email: info@violencefreeco.org

No More: Campaign to End Domestic Violence

"*Women should know that love doesn't abuse you. It shouldn't hurt you. Love cannot be redefined into 'He only hit me once, I'll let it slide.' Love is happiness, not being neglectful, caring, being respectful, providing, having standards, kindness, standing up for the right things.*"

— Jahmene Douglas

Books and Articles

The following represent just a few of many outstanding books and important articles on domestic and intimate partner violence

TESSA: "12 Things You Can Do to Help Combat Intimate Partner Violence." Available online at tessacs.org/12-ways-to-help.

S.G. Smith, X Zhang, K.C. Basile, et al. *The National Intimate Partner and Sexual Violence Survey* (NISVS): 2015 Data Brief. Available online at CDC.gov.

Megan L. Evans, MD, MPH, Margo Lindauer, JD, and Maureen E. Farrell, MD. "A Pandemic within a Pandemic - Intimate Partner Violence during Covid-19." *New England Journal of Medicine*, December 10, 2020.

S. Fielding, "In Quarantine with an Abuser: Surge in Domestic Violence Reports Linked to Coronavirus." *The Guardian*: April 3, 2020.

Lundy Bancroft, *When Dad Hurts Mom: Helping Your Children Heal the Wounds of Witnessing Abuse*. Berkeley: 2004.

Lundy Bancroft, *Why Does He Do That: Inside the Minds of Angry and Controlling Men*. G.P. Putnam's Sons: 2002.

Barry Goldstein, *Scared to Leave, Afraid to Stay: Paths from Family Violence to Safety*. Robert D. Reed Publishers: 2002.

Barry Goldstein, *The Quincy Solution: Stop Domestic Violence and Save $500 Billion*. Robert D. Reed Publishers, 2014.

Judith Lewis Herman, *Trauma and Recovery: The Aftermath of Violence – From Domestic Abuse to Political Terror*. Basic Books: 1992.

Rachel Louise Snyder, *No Visible Bruises: What We Don't Know about Domestic Violence Can Kill Us.* Bloomsbury: 2019.

Eleanor Weiss, *Surviving Domestic Violence.* Volcano Press: 2004.

Tara Westover, *Educated.* Penguin Random House: 2019.

From Your Publisher's Editor

My husband, Bob Reed, owner of Robert D. Reed Publishers, has been publishing books for over fifty years. All his life, he has chosen books that he says, "make this a better world one book at a time," and many of these books have addressed social issues. In our library at www.rdrpublishers.com, we have several books on abuse: bullying, child abuse, sexual abuse, ritual abuse, religious abuse, genocide, and domestic violence. Publishing this book, *Domestic Violence: Tragedy and Hope*, was a natural YES.

On a personal level, this book resonates with me because of my personal experiences. I grew up with what I would call emotional deprivation and have been married three times. I experienced domestic violence in my second marriage, which is the theme of my poem, "Abuse Is Not an Option."

I share this poem because 1) I resonated with every word in this book because I once was a victim of domestic violence, and 2) I think it is important that I live my life with authenticity and not hide in shame because I "let bad stuff happen to me."

We are all on a journey of self-discovery and healing. Had I "lucked out" and stayed married to the same man for fifty years, who knows what I would have done professionally or what kinds of personal-growth work I would have done.

What I do know is that my history led me to where I am today. Following my second divorce and a lot of deep personal-growth work, I met Bob. And here I am, living a life of constant gratitude to be happily married to an absolutely wonderful man – who happens to be a book publisher – editing books, designing book covers and promotional materials, and now even contributing to this book with one of my poems.

~ Cleone Lyvonne Reed

Abuse is Not an Option

I got remarried when I was thirty-nine
And expected life to be really fine.
Who would have guessed it would be hell?
Domestic violence, I could not foretell.
Twenty-one episodes in that first year.
Every day I was full of fear.
I didn't dare go to work
For fear he would again go berserk.

The worst was when he tried to choke me.
Sensitive thereafter my neck would be.
A kick in the stomach landed me on the ground.
Scared stiff to the neighbors I'd be found.
Grabbing me often by the wrist
Leaving me bruises with his fist.
His rampages were all about control
And on my mental health they took a toll.

I didn't want another divorce
But just to get on a better course.
I told him henceforth every time he touched me
Lovingly it absolutely had to be.
He changed and was no longer rough,
But the marriage was still not good enough.
His temper and language were full of anger
And life still had an element of danger.

I told 32 people I was getting a divorce before I told him.
I knew I couldn't blurt it out in a whim.
The fear was he would kill me with his gun

And then kill himself when he was done.
So out of the marriage and on my own
At age fifty, two thousand miles were flown.
I wanted to heal and create a better life
And be a healthy, loving man's wife.

Forgiveness of him became a goal.
He had stolen a big piece of my soul.
After some work, I labeled myself a survivor.
Was this doing my consciousness a favor?
It was at least beyond the victim state
But I wanted to thrive and move beyond that fate.
So I went on an intensive healing journey
That took me deeper than I wanted to be.

Painful, it was like a wild roller coaster ride
One minute happy, the next wanting to hide.
Some would say I set my sights too high.
But I didn't think they were pie in the sky.
More than getting a Master's Degree,
The Avatar Course is what really set me free.
What I integrated can never be taken away.
My soul transformed; the changes are here to stay.

Then meeting Bob when I was fifty-seven
Felt like I had maybe gone to heaven!
Later, when I was sixty-two, I married Bob.
It wasn't too late to land my heart-throb.
We are viewed as compatible by everyone.
He is supportive, loving, generous, caring and fun.
Gratitude fills my whole being every day and night.
He is truly a star in my eyes, shining ever so bright.

*We all like to think that if we were
the victims of domestic abuse we'd up
and leave – but it's not always as easy or
straightforward as that. Women stay with abusive
partners for all kinds of reasons – they love them,
they fear them, they have children with them,
they believe they can change them or they simply
have no where else to go.*

— Kate Thornton

About the Author

Frances T. Pilch is Professor Emeritus in Political Science at the United States Air Force Academy. She has written extensively on violence against women, especially as a weapon of war, and on genocide. Her most recent book is *Invisible: Surviving the Cambodian Genocide – the Memoirs of Mac and Simone Leng*, Robert D. Reed Publishers.

Nowhere in the world is a woman safe from violence. The strengthening of global commitment to counteract this plague is a movement whose time has come.

—Asha-Rose Migiro

Notes

NOTES

NOTES

NOTES